The FRUGAL Science Teacher

STRATEGIES AND ACTIVITIES

6-9

The FRUGAL Science Teacher

STRATEGIES AND ACTIVITIES

Linda Froschauer, editor

National Science Teachers Association

National Science Teachers Association

Claire Reinburg, Director
Jennifer Horak, Managing Editor
Andrew Cocke, Senior Editor
Judy Cusick, Senior Editor
Wendy Rubin, Associate Editor
Amy America, Book Acquisitions Coordinator

SCIENCE AND CHILDREN
Linda Froschauer, Editor
Valynda Mayes, Managing Editor
Stephanie Andersen, Associate Editor

SCIENCE SCOPE
Inez Liftig, Editor
Kenneth L. Roberts, Managing Editor
Janna Palliser, Consulting Editor

THE SCIENCE TEACHER
Steve Metz, Editor
Stephanie Liberatore, Managing Editor
Meg Streker, Assistant Editor

ART AND DESIGN
Will Thomas Jr., Director
Tim French, Cover and Interior Design

PRINTING AND PRODUCTION
Catherine Lorrain, Director

NATIONAL SCIENCE TEACHERS ASSOCIATION
Francis Q. Eberle, PhD, Executive Director
David Beacom, Publisher

Library of Congress Cataloging-in-Publication Data
The frugal science teacher, 6-9 : strategies and activities / edited by Linda Froschauer. -- 1st ed.
    p. cm.
 ISBN 978-1-936137-01-5
 1. Science--Study and teaching (Middle school)--Activity programs. 2. Science--Methodology--Study and teaching (Middle
school) I. Froschauer, Linda.
 Q181.F838 2009
 507.1'2--dc22
                          2009047861

 eISBN 978-1-936137-77-0

CONTENTS

PART 3.   TEACHING STRATEGIES THAT MAXIMIZE THE SCIENCE BUDGET

Projects

Games

Posters and Cartoons

Newsletters

Stations

Current Events

PART 4.   INSTRUCTIONAL LESSONS THAT MAXIMIZE THE SCIENCE BUDGET

PART 5.   FUNDS AND MATERIALS

Preface

by Linda Froschauer

frugal *(froo'gal) adj. Practicing or marked by economy, as in the expenditure of money or the use of material resources. See synonym at* sparing. *2. Costing little; inexpensive.*

—The American Heritage Dictionary

Frugality practically defines how we as teachers approach provisioning our classrooms. (I half expected to see a picture of a science teacher next to the entry!) We cleverly create learning opportunities with limited resources and have amazing aptitudes for stretching shrinking funds and doing more with limited resources. Still, we find ourselves augmenting school and district funds with our own dollars, digging into our own pockets to purchase equipment and other essentials. A quick web search suggests that K–12 teachers spend between $475 and $1,500—per year—on classroom materials. And we do this willingly because we know it makes a difference in our students' learning.

In an issue of *Science Scope* devoted to limited classroom resources, editor Inez Liftig expressed concern about giving tacit approval to the expectations that teachers should spend their own money to outfit their classrooms: "I wanted to be very sure that we did not send the wrong message about whether or not science teachers should spend their own money to support instruction. . . . Parents and school districts should not expect teachers to pay for equipment and supplies from personal funds, and we should not have to choose between doing them at all" (Liftig 2007, p. 6). I share her concern, but my intent here is not to lecture or opine. Rather, I hope this volume provides a valuable reference at a time when we all need to be resourceful.

To collect all of the articles, books, websites, and organizations that can help you save money is an impossible feat. Not only is there a tremendous quantity of available resources, but the information also changes rapidly and is best pursued through internet searches. Therefore, you will not see lists of websites, grants, and "free" opportunities in this book. Rather, you will find a collection of inspiring articles and book chapters that will provide you and your students with valuable, standards-based learning opportunities that can also serve as springboards to additional investigations. The authors detail untapped resources for materials, reimagined uses for items you already have at home or school, inexpensive workarounds to costly classroom projects, and creative activities that require only free or inexpensive materials.

In addition, many articles and chapters include suggestions for further reading that may expand on the ideas discussed, apply a similar learning tool in a different way, or revise a particular activity for use with different grade ranges. These additional resources are available through the NSTA Science Store (*www. nsta.org/store*), for free or little cost.

A WORD ABOUT ORGANIZATION

This book comprises five categories, or overarching strategies, for thinking about how to conduct science investigations without spending a great deal of money—either your own funds or those acquired through your district budget.

Student-Created Constructions

When students build their own equipment or create their own models, they have a greater connection to the overall experience, thus enhancing learning. An amazing number of investigations can be developed with a single piece of paper, throwaway items, or dollar-store finds. You already may be familiar with more traditional student constructions, such as paper airplanes, and the lessons they convey. Think how much more students could learn from building roller coasters or paper towers.

Teacher-Created Constructions and Repurposed Materials

Science teachers are great savers of materials. We check out sale bins in stores and rinse out used containers. We collect soda bottles, aluminum cans, shoe boxes, scraps of wood, odd lots of rubber bands, old CDs . . . anything that may possibly be useful in our classrooms. This section suggests ways to put those materials to good use in two general categories: repurposing materials that we have collected and building equipment for student use from free or inexpensive components.

Teaching Strategies That Maximize the Science Budget

There are many ways to reorganize our instructional approaches that enable quality learning to occur at reduced cost. The articles in this section provide suggestions on how to engage students through a variety of strategies. Although the strategies are explained within the context of a specific content area, they can serve as creative inspiration as you consider how to adjust lessons in *any* content area. Creating project materials, playing games, drawing cartoons, developing class newsletters, using learning stations, and tapping into current events all require minimal financial investments but provide enriched experiences for students. Many of these ideas also integrate other subject areas to provide broader curriculum impact.

Instructional Lessons That Maximize the Science Budget

The fourth section offers a collection of life science, Earth science, and physical science and chemistry investigations. They are specific to a given content area but utilize materials that may stimulate ideas for innovative activities with any subject matter. You can use them as they are or modify them to fit your curriculum. Several articles highlight the use of outdoor spaces around your school site that are ideal for scientific investigations.

Funds and Materials

Even after implementing the ideas in this book, you may still have classroom needs that prove too costly to be fulfilled through your budget (or pocket). This section presents suggestions for how to acquire those additional funds.

ADDITIONAL RESOURCES FROM NSTA

In this volume, I have culled some of the most useful NSTA print resources for maximizing your classroom dollars. However, NSTA also provides a variety of free electronic resources that are available for members and nonmembers alike to improve both teaching and learning.

e-Publications

Individual articles from *Science and Children*, *Science Scope*, and *The Science Teacher*, as well as chapters from NSTA Press books, are available in electronic format from NSTA's online Science Store (*www.nsta.org/store*). Many of these—at least two articles per journal issue and one chapter per book—are free to everyone. (The balance of articles is free to NSTA members and available for a small fee to nonmembers.)

Teachers and administrators can also keep up with what's happening in the world of science education by signing up for free weekly and monthly e-mail newsletters (*http://www.nsta.org/publications/enewsletters. aspx*). *NSTA Express* delivers the latest news and information about science education, including legislative updates, weekly. Every month *Science Class* offers teachers theme-based content in the grade band of their choosing—elementary, middle level, or high school. News articles, journal articles from the NSTA archives, and appropriate book content support each theme. *Scientific Principals*, also monthly, provides a science toolbox full of new ideas and practical applications for elementary school principals.

Learning Center

Anyone—teachers, student teachers, principals, or parents—can open a free account at the NSTA Learning Center, a repository of electronic materials to help enhance both content and pedagogical knowledge. By creating a personal library, users can easily access, sort, and even share a variety of resources:

Science Objects are free two-hour online, interactive, inquiry-based content modules that help teachers better understand the science content they teach. New objects are continually added, but the wide-ranging list of topics includes forces and motion, the universe, the solar system, energy, coral ecosystems, plate tectonics, the rock cycle, the ocean's effect on weather and climate, and science safety.

SciGuides are online resources that help teachers integrate the web into their classroom instruction. Each guide consists of approximately 100 standards-aligned, web-accessible resources, accompanying lesson plans, teacher vignettes that describe the lessons, and more. Although most SciGuides must be purchased, there is always one available at no charge.

SciPacks combine the content of three to five Science Objects with access to a content expert, a pedagogical component to help teachers understand common student misconceptions, and the chance to pass a final assessment and receive a certificate. Yearlong SciPack subscriptions must also be purchased, but one SciPack is always available for free.

Anyone may participate in a live, 90-minute web seminar for no-cost professional development experiences. Participants interact with renowned experts, NSTA Press authors, scientists, engineers, and other education specialists. Seminar archives are also available on the NSTA website and can be accessed at any time.

Particularly popular web seminars are also offered in smaller pieces as podcasts that can be downloaded and listened to on the go. These 2- to 60-minute portable segments include mini-tutorials on specific content and ideas for classroom activities.

Grants and Awards

NSTA cosponsors the prestigious Toyota Tapestry Grants for Teachers (*www.nsta.org/pd/tapestry*), offering funds to K–12 science teachers for innovative projects that enhance science education in the school or school district. Fifty large grants and at least 20 mini-grants—totaling $550,000—are awarded each year. NSTA also supports nearly 20 other teacher award programs, many of which recognize and fund outstanding classroom programs (*www.nsta.org/about/awards.aspx*).

You may not save hundreds of dollars a year by following the recommendations found in this book. You will, however, find creative ways to keep expenses down and stretch your funds while building student understanding. . . . And perhaps you will be inspired to invent your own low cost constructions, develop even more inexpensive student activities, find additional uses for everyday items, or uncover a wealth of new resources for obtaining classroom materials.

Reference

Liftig, I. 2007. Never cut corners on safety. *Science Scope* 30 (6): 6–7.

PART

Student-Created
Constructions

Chapter 1

Geology on a Sand Budget

Students Use Sand to Model Earth Science Processes and Features

by Jacqueline Kane

Earth science teachers know how frustrating it can be to spend hundreds of dollars on three-dimensional (3-D) models of Earth's geologic features and then use the models for only a few class periods. To avoid emptying an already limited science budget, teachers can use a simple alternative to the expensive 3-D models—sand. Modeling geologic processes and features with sand is an effective way for teachers to promote student understanding of Earth science topics, quickly assess students' prior knowledge, and identify common misconceptions.

Sand activities serve as a medium to shift the emphases in science teaching, as described in the *National Science Education Standards* (NRC 1996, p. 27). Sand activities allow teachers to access student knowledge and understanding while they are engaged in the learning process.

AN EFFECTIVE MEDIUM

Earth science 3-D processes are difficult to grasp using two-dimensional (2-D) media. Lab activity often is reduced to graphing, or paper models at best, while 3-D modeling generally is demonstrated by teachers without student interaction. Computer simulations are helpful, but the images are flat.

Sand, however, allows students to directly model geologic processes and features. Sand is an efficient instructional medium for other reasons as well. The equipment is inexpensive and easily stored (or simply discarded); activities are brief and adaptable; and preparation is minimal (Figure 1, p. 4). A few safety precautions should be noted when using sand in a school laboratory (Figure 1), but cleanup is quick and easy when typical laboratory behavior is enforced. Assessment is instant and paperless!

MODELING EXAMPLES

Several geological features can be modeled with sand (Figure 2, p. 5). In my classroom, students model glacial features and sand dunes after discussing river and glacial erosion (Figure 2A, p. 5). Using wet sand contained in paint trays, students first model *nonglaciated* (V-shaped) stream-eroded valleys by molding the sand into steep-sided valleys. Then, students simulate glaciers moving down V-shaped valleys by pushing a small plastic bag of sand down the modeled valleys—*glaciated* (U-shaped) valleys form. The area formed between two parallel valleys is an *arête* (knife-sharp ridge). If students push a third simulated glacier down and away from the ridge at the valley head in an opposing direction to the first two glaciated valleys—and erode a valley more or less perpendicular to the arête—a three-sided peak, called a *horn* (like the Matterhorn) forms. Similarly, other features, such as *hanging valleys*, appear above the main valley. Farther down the valleys students form glacial depositional features, such as *moraines*, and the snake-like remains of streams form under glaciers, called *eskers*. Students also make sand dunes in the same way as the glacier features, by carving and building wet sand. Examples of these sand dune types are available on the internet (see On the Web, p. 6).

I also explain topographic maps to students, give them a topographical map (Figure 2B, p. 5), and ask them to make a sand model. Having students interpret the map allows them to demonstrate their knowledge of the meaning of contour lines learned and gives me an opportunity to assess their understanding of the material. In all the sand modeling activities, I walk around the room quizzing students with questions such as "What caused that waterfall cliff at the hanging valley?" "How can you tell which way the wind was blowing in your barchans sand dune model?" "What does your model tell you about the direction of compressional forces with your fault?" and "How will building a dam on that river affect human lives upriver?"

Understanding develops as students become more accustomed to building the sand models. Modeling establishes a sound basis to discuss more complex issues and to advance into 2-D representations of data such as satellite images. Higher-level thinking skills naturally evolve in related discussions of natural hazards and environmental concerns because students have a solid understanding of the basics enhanced by 3-D sand models.

ADDITIONAL APPLICATIONS

Authentic problems can have "sandy" solutions. For example, one looming environmental problem is groundwater contamination. Engineers use a method for removing particular contaminants in certain soils before they reach the water table. In class, I demonstrate a well-accepted ground restoration process—soil vapor extraction. I introduce an acidic liquid contaminant (vinegar) into a flask of sand (the ground) and then lower the vapor pressure over the sand with a vacuum pump, which allows much of the liquid to vaporize and be extracted. (If no vacuum pump is available, low pressure can be achieved using an aspirator attached to a water faucet.) A simple colorimetric method will confirm the contaminant's removal if the extracted vinegar vapor is bubbled through a weak solution of NaOH and phenolphthalein indicator.

Figure 1

Preparing for the sand activities

Purchasing Information

(for approximately seven groups of two to four students)

- 1 gal. plastic paint buckets for storing and carrying sand
- Paint stirrer for mixing water into the dry sand
- One 14 L bag of sandbox sand
- 7 plastic paint trays (flimsy but cheap)
- Plastic spoons for carving (about 30)
- About 2.5 cm x 5 cm paper cutouts for labels
- Box of toothpicks for labels
- Dust pan, whisk, and floor brooms

Basic Setup for Land Feature Modeling

- In a mixing bucket, mix about a 250 ml beaker of water into 2 L of sand and stir with a paint stick.
- Scoop out about 2 L of moist sand from the mixing bucket into each paint tray.
- Give paper labels and toothpicks to each student group.

Modeling Tips

- Write out specific required qualities such as "wind side of dune should be less steep."
- Base evaluations on evidence of understanding rather than on quality of model.
- Require verbal explanation and revision after noting mistakes.

Safety Measures

- Premix water with sand to prevent sand dust from permeating the room (some children react to fine dust particles).
- Use low-clay-content sand such as sandbox sand.
- Students must wear goggles to protect their eyes.
- Monitor a "no sand in air or on the floor" policy.
- Protect tables with old posters.
- Remove computers and calculators.
- Require students to rinse hands and equipment in a water bucket before washing.

The solution turns from pink to colorless, indicating a partial removal of the vinegar contaminant.

In addition to modeling with sand, students can study sand up close thanks to my growing collection. Students are aware of my fascination with sand, and they bring sand samples into class from all over the United States. I keep a binocular microscope and a variety of sand samples readily available. Sand is amazingly varied; under a microscope students can

Figure 2

Modeling geologic features

A. Glacial Features and Sand Dunes
Directions

Using your tray of wet sand and a spoon, model the following features. If you cannot make all features at one time, you may make each one separately and have it checked by the teacher before destroying it and making the next. Make and place paper and toothpick labels on your features. Be prepared to discuss how the features were formed in nature. After your group has discussed your model with the teacher, remove and throw out your labels, carry the tray with the spoons back to the supply table, and rinse your hands in the rinse water bucket before washing in the sink. Sweep up any spilled sand on the table with the small broom and spilled sand on the floor with the floor broom.

Features to model

Glacial

Nonglaciated (V-shaped) valley
Glaciated (U-shaped) valley
Cirque
Horn
Arête
Hanging valley
Drumlin
End moraine
Lateral moraine
Little lake
Outwash plain

Dunes

Barchan
Longitudinal
Parabolic
Star
Barchanoid
Transverse

B. Topographic Model
Directions

Using your tray of wet sand, make a 3-D model of the topographic map below. Identify the highest and lowest elevations, which way the stream is flowing, and which side of the hill is steepest. If the area flooded to 20 m, what feature would be formed?

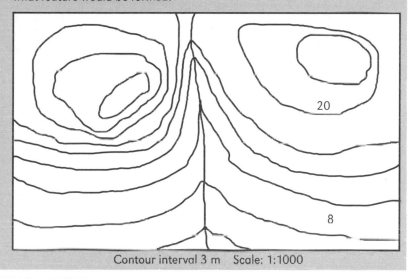

Contour interval 3 m   Scale: 1:1000

---

identify quartz, mica, and feldspar grains for mineral study. This naturally leads into an introduction of optical mineralogy.

FAMILIAR AND EFFECTIVE

Many students excel with these laboratory activities. When students build 3-D models, I can immediately tell who understands the geologic concepts. Therefore, I can correct or modify misconceptions before they are learned.

Every activity can be altered to the uniqueness of a class and time restrictions, and to reflect current events such as the Mars Rover exploration and weather-related calamities. Also, teachers with expertise in biology, chemistry, or physics can use sand as a medium for supporting cell parts, purifying water,

showing specific heat concepts through the heating of dry and wet sand, or demonstrating physical and chemical changes. For example, the acid-neutralizing capacity of various types of sand can be investigated through a simple activity that connects chemistry and Earth science. This activity is particularly effective if sand can be obtained from local sources and also from other geographic locations. Students place 3–5 cm of sand in a Styrofoam cup and then add about 25 ml of prepared "acid rain" solution that has a pH around 4–5. After stirring the sand-acid mixture, students retest the solution's acidity, either directly in the cup or after it has been allowed to percolate through the sand and pass into another container through small holes punched into the bottom of the cup. Many sands produce very little neutralizing capacity, though limestone sands—like those found in Florida and the Caribbean, for example—often return the acidity to nearly neutral pH 7. Students discover that where the sand comes from makes a difference, and that acid rain can have a different effect on the various soil types found in different parts of the country.

Sand modeling is simple, familiar, and creative. Modeling with this medium has effectively resulted in my academically diverse students looking forward to class. I also like sand because there are as many modeling applications as the creative mind can envision. Learning with sand establishes fond memories—who has not enjoyed squishing sand between fingers, building sand castles at the beach, or contemplating the sands of time?

Reference

National Research Council (NRC). 1996. *National science education standards*. Washington, DC: National Academies Press.

This article first appeared in the September 2004 issue of The Science Teacher.

On the Web

The following websites offer valuable information pertaining to the activities in this article:

- **TerraServer USA**
  An online database that provides free maps and aerial photographs of the United States
  http://terraserver-usa.com

- **Explore Nature: Geology**
  A good reference for national park geology
  www.nature.nps.gov/geology

- **San Francisco Estuary Institute**
  An excellent reference on map interpretation
  www.sfei.org/ecoatlas/GIS/MapInterpretation/TopographicMapInterp.html

- **Visible Earth**
  A search engine and directory of pictures of Earth from NASA
  http://visibleearth.nasa.gov

Chapter 2
Roller Coaster Inquiry

by Carla Johnson

In an effort to move away from more structured, step-by-step physics activities, I designed the following problem-based project to kick off the school year. The project, which centers on roller coaster design, engages students in learning about physics and activates their prior knowledge in an open-inquiry environment. The activity also gets students involved with inquiry during the first few weeks of class. Students are presented with an authentic problem before receiving content instruction, they learn about the content through group interaction and by coming up with a solution to the problem.

THE PROBLEM

For this project, students receive a letter (drafted by the teacher) from their local amusement park that solicits design proposals from physics students. The letter asks students to create small-scale models and proposals for a new roller coaster that will be added to the park. A timeline is provided for each piece of the proposal. The teacher explains that students will work collaboratively in teams of two to four. After student teams are created, the planning process begins.

PLANNING

Groups first are asked to brainstorm and list qualities that make a good roller coaster. Before beginning work on the coaster, students are required to develop a blueprint in class of what they want their ride to do and how they want it to look. At this point, students also should determine a name for their roller coaster.

Once students have a completed design that has been approved by the teacher, they begin constructing the model—a small-scale marble roller coaster (the marble represents the car)

MODEL CONSTRUCTION

The model roller coaster should be no larger than 0.6 m × 1.2 m. Students can create working loops and corkscrews with poster board and other materials from home, such as plastic tubing and wood.

This same activity can be completed using just poster board, if it is difficult for students to bring materials from home. Each group needs three pieces of poster board, one for the base of the roller coaster and the other two to construct the tracks. The cost per group for completing this activity is approximately $1. Using recycled poster board materials reduces the cost even further and also makes an important point about the value of recycling. Masking tape can be used to fasten the "beams" and "track" together, and a marble is used to test the track.

TEACHER AS FACILITATOR

During the activity, the teacher facilitates planning and construction and asks guiding questions to help students understand why some things do not work as planned. Questions might include "How much potential and kinetic energy is required to 'power' the marble coaster?" or "What effect does friction have on the marble?" This type of experience allows students to take charge of their learning and to construct understandings from their interactions with group members and the teacher.

FOLLOWING UP

With proper advance planning, this activity can be completed in one or two class periods and can be expanded in many ways. For example, the final product can be painted and the surrounding areas of the park decorated with grass, trees, and people to give an accurate picture of what the actual roller coaster would look like in the park.

Students also can prepare video presentations (at school) to demonstrate their roller coasters and "market" them to the executives at the amusement park. Students can market their coasters in a commercial-style format and provide jingles and catchy phrases to help their presentations stand out. The teacher also can ask students to complete written proposals with the final project, requiring students to estimate costs for the actual construction of the roller coasters and prepare budgets using resources form the internet.

MULTIPLE ASSESSMENTS

Evaluation of the project is completed in several ways, depending on how much time the teacher has for assessment. Students can be assessed each day as the teacher interacts with them and questions them on the physics concepts associated with their models. The written proposals and budgets can also be evaluated for grades. At the conclusion of the project, students should be assessed on not only their presetation skills but also content knowledge demonstrated in the presentation.

This article first appeared in the September 2004 issue of The Science Teacher.

Chapter 3
Ever Fly a Tetrahedron?

by Kenneth King

Figure 1

Forces acting on a kite

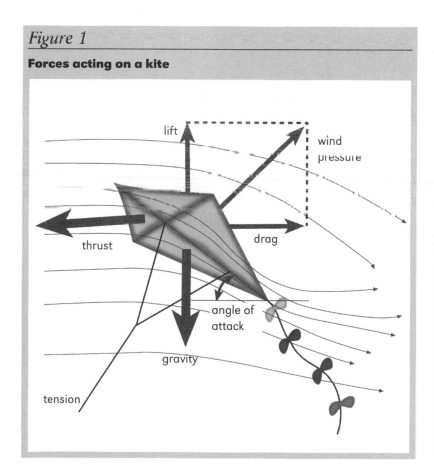

lift

wind pressure

thrust

drag

angle of attack

gravity

tension

Few activities capture the spirit of spring like flying a kite. Watching a kite dance and sail across a cloud-spotted sky is not only a visually appealing experience, it also provides a foundation for studies in science and mathematics.

THE SCIENCE OF KITES

Put simply, a kite is an airfoil surface that flies when the forces of lift and thrust are greater than the

Further Reading

- "Taking Flight With an Inquiry Approach," from the September 2008 issue of *Science Scope*

chapter 3

Teacher Notes for Activities
- This lesson takes multiple days to complete—one or two days to model and construct a single cell, one day to construct multiple cells, and an additional day to attach tissue paper and construct tetrahedral kites.
- Arrange for permission (if needed) to conduct flying investigations during the days following the construction of the kites. Based on characteristics of the class, additional adult (parent or guardian) assistance may be warranted.
- A large open field is most appropriate for kite-flying activities. Compile a set of kite-flying rules as a whole class, voting on the rules and consequences for violating safety considerations. (See safety guidelines on p. 12.)
- Individual tetrahedrons stack easily and take up very little counter space.
- Student-constructed kites (made of 4 to 16 cells) are lightweight and can be hung from ceiling tile brackets, keeping the kites out of the way until needed. It may be advisable to consult with your custodial staff regarding any fire code concerns with hanging paper objects from the ceiling.
- Remind timekeepers to keep the group aware of the need to reel in kites well before the class has to return inside.
- Build some sample tetrahedrons at different stages of construction as visual aids for students.

Preconstruction Student Questions
- Which geometric solid has the smallest number of sides?
- How are triangles—single and multiple units—used in the construction of various structures such as bridges and towers?
- How does making an airplane larger allow it to carry larger and heavier objects?

Materials
(For each team of two students)
- 24 plastic drinking straws
- Scissors
- Glue
- 100 m of kite string
- 100 m of fishing line (approximately 30–60 lb. test)
- 2 sheets of wrapping tissue, (approximately 24 in. x 36 in., standard size)
- Darning needle (to assist in passing fishing line through straws)
- Approximately 10 cm of masking tape (to hold straws in place while constructing tetrahedrons)
- Astrolabe
- Cardboard template for cutting tissue paper to proper size
- Wind meter (optional)

Procedure
1. View the sample construction materials assembled by your teacher, including

   - a tetrahedron constructed of straws;
   - a tetrahedron with tissue paper covering two of the four sides; and
   - a tetrahedron kite, constructed with four tissue-covered tetrahedral cells organized into a single, larger tetrahedron.

Figure 2

Constructing kite cells

1. Run string through three straws, arranged as above.

2. Continue on with the string through two additional straws, arranged as above.

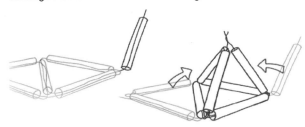

3. Take the string through one more straw.

4. Form a pyramid out of the straws and tie off the lead end of the strings.

2. Work with your teammate to construct your own four-cell tetrahedron kite by following along as your teacher demonstrates the proper threading technique. Begin by taping three straws to the tabletop in an equilateral triangle. Thread fishing line onto the needle and string it through the straws as shown in Figure 2.

3. Use the template in Figure 3 to cut out a tissue-paper covering for two sides of the tetrahedron. Cover only two sides of the tetrahedron. Glue the covering over the frame, wrapping the excess materials around the straw framework.

4. Repeat steps 1 through 3 to create a total of four tetrahedrons (see Figure 1, p. 13). Once you have the hang of it, continue to construct tetrahedrons in your spare time at home or at school until you have assembled 16.

5. Try to arrange your four tetrahedrons to create one larger tetrahedron. Once you have a successful arrangement, notify the teacher.

6. Observe how your teacher has arranged the four tetrahedrons at the front of the room so that the two covered faces of each are aligned the same way (see Figure 4). Arrange your tetrahedrons in this manner and bind them together at the corners with fishing line to hold them in place. Make sure all knots are pulled tight.

7. Create a bridle for your kite to which you will attach the kite string. First attach one end of a string to the apex of the pyramid and the other to one of the base corners. Attach one end of a second string to one corner of the base of the top tetrahedron and the other end across the front of the tetrahedron to the second corner (see Figure 5, p. 13). Tie the two strings together where they cross. The kite string will be attached at this intersection. In general the strings should be taut and the bridle should be close to your kite.

8. Before going outside, review your kite-flying safety rules. Note that you should avoid running around with the kite, and instead allow the wind to lift the kite. If a wind meter is available, try to determine the minimum amount of wind needed to lift your kite.

9. As a class, carefully transport your kites to the area designated for flying. Attach 8 to 10 m of string to the bridle. One person on your team holds the string while the other holds the kite off the ground. Once the kite is released, assuming there is enough wind, the kite should fly like an inverted pyramid with one point downward. It is the job of the student who released the kite to take an angle measurement with

Figure 3

Tissue-paper template

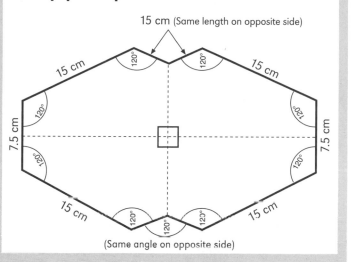

the astrolabe, which you will use later to determine the altitude reached by the kite.

10. Fly the kite for 10 to 12 minutes before returning to class. Take turns holding the string and taking astrolabe measurements.

11. Return to class and use your astrolabe reading to determine the height reached by the kite. Discuss with your teammate how the kite handled, any problems you had using the astrolabe, and any other observations you made during the flight.

Designing an Experiment

Now that you have familiarized yourself with the characteristics of the tetrahedron kite, design an experiment to determine how changing one variable in the kite's design affects its performance. For example, you could build a kite using

- heavier tissue paper or a different kind of covering, such as newspaper or cling wrap;
- 16 tetrahedron cells instead of 4; or
- the same number of cells but in a different arrangement.

Present your experimental design to the teacher for approval, including a sample of the data table you will use. Obtain any additional materials needed, such as a stopwatch, weights, and covering materials prior to the next flight.

continued on page 12

Flying Tetrahedrons, continued

Safety

- Fly your kite where it will not cause a hazard to yourself or others. Kites should be flown in an open area, away from people, roads, and obstructions.
- Since kites and kite lines can be dangerous, safety should always be your primary concern. Be aware of your environment. If there is ever any question of safety, fly the kite in another location or on another day.
- Never fly your kite near power lines. If your kite becomes tangled in power lines, *leave it there* and notify your utility company of the situation.
- Never fly near cars.
- Never fly near an airport.
- Never fly in stormy weather or when a storm is approaching.
- Never fly over people.
- Avoid kite-eating trees.
- Always keep a safe distance from other fliers.

Tip: You can prevent problems by restricting the length of the line that you use. Make it shorter than the distance to the nearest obstacle!

Notes: The most frequent injury during kite flying is sunburn. Be sure to protect yourself from the Sun with hats, sunglasses, and sunscreen.

The second most frequent injury during kite flying is a cut or burn from the kite line. Do not allow the line to zip through your fingers. Do not use monofilament fishing line. For large kites, protect your hands by wearing leather gloves. These safety rules are found in Kites in the Classroom (*www.aka.kite.org/data/ download/pdf/Manuals/kitc.pdf*) and have been reprinted with permission from the American Kitefliers Association (*www.aka.kite.org*). AKA invites you to join them for National Kite Month (*www.nationalkitemonth. org*) in April. Register your kite-flying activity for a chance to win some kites and accessories.

forces of drag and gravity. In between flying and crashing to the ground are a variety of swoops, wiggles, pitches, yaws, and rolls that show the kite seeking a balance among the set of conflicting forces.

A kite creates an obstacle to the normal airflow (Peters 2001), which causes the air to change direction and speed. The air flows across one surface faster than it moves across the other side of that surface. The difference in speeds produces a pressure differential, resulting in lift in the direction of the surface with faster moving air. As air pressure can be altered by changing the kite's angle of attack, the changes in air speed result in changes in air pressure, which cause the kite to produce greater lift (see Figure 1, p. 9).

CONSTRUCTING A KITE

The student activity in this article explains how to build a tetrahedron kite. The kites can then be used as the basis of a student-designed inquiry. Using tetrahedron cells to construct a kite offers numerous advantages. In principle, a kite constructed of tetrahedrons can be built to any size, simply by using combinations of tetrahedral cells. The cells are rigid and do not require extra bracing to maintain their shape. This results in kites that become stronger and more stable as they increase in size without additional bracing or support.

Constructing the kites requires plastic drinking straws, tissue paper, fishing line, glue, scissors, and a darning needle. An example of the basic tetrahedron cell is shown in Figure 2 (p. 10). Fishing line is threaded through the straws to maintain the tetrahedron's structure. The four surfaces are then covered in tissue paper (see Figure 3, p. 11, for tissue-paper template). Multiple tetrahedrons can be arranged to form even larger tetrahedrons. A set of four cells provides a good introduction to the operation of a tetrahedral kite (see Figure 4). More advanced or ambitious investigations would require a larger number of tetrahedral cells.

This is an inexpensive activity. For a class of 30 students, I spent $7 on straws, $6 on tissue paper, and a few more dollars on glue, fishing line, darning needles, and kite string. If your budget allows, you can experiment with graphite rods, ripstop nylon, and other high-tech materials. Visit *www.intothewind.com* for instructions on making more permanent tetrahedral kites.

TESTING KITES

Testing the kites provides an opportunity to engage in hypothesis formulation and technological design studies. Students may be inspired by the work of Alexander Graham Bell, who investigated the structure, operation, and lifting capacity of tetrahedral kites at the end of the 19th and beginning of the 20th centuries (Bell 1903).

One of the advantages of kite cells is that they can be quickly and easily modified so students can test many variables. For example, students can easily construct kites to compare the lifting power of a 4-cell kite to that of a 16-cell kite, or they can alter the arrangement of the kite cells to see how designs affect stability.

IMPLEMENTING THE ACTIVITIES

Before getting started, your students need to know how to create and implement their own experiments and control variables. They should also be able to use an astrolabe to indirectly measure the height of the kites. (Instructions for building and using an astrolabe can be found on p. 22 of the April 1997 issue of *Science Scope*, which is also available free to NSTA members from the online archive at *www.nsta.org/middleschool*.) Two other useful resources for preparing your students for these activities are *Height-O-Meters* (Sneider 1988) and *Experimenting With Model Rockets* (Sneider 1989), both from Lawrence Hall of Science.

ASSESSMENT

When assessing this activity, you should check to see if

- the kite construction demonstrates care and craftsmanship,
- the team consistently observed safety rules,
- a sound experimental design was created and followed, and
- an appropriate data table was created and meaningful data collected.

CONCLUSION

Interdisciplinary instruction works best when the experiences help students learn content and processes in a broadly based context. Whether arranged according to themes, skills, or concepts, interdisciplinary instruction offers the opportunity to engage a subject and many related experiences in greater depth and a more meaningful context.

ACKNOWLEDGMENT

Thanks to Chad Juehring for the original artwork included in this article.

References

Bell, A.G. 1903. The tetrahedral principle in kite structure. *National Geographic* 44: 219–251.

National Research Council (NRC). 1996. *National science education standards*. Washington, DC: National Academies Press.

Peters, P. 2001. Why do kites fly? Retrieved on November 4, 2002 from *www.win.tue.nl/~pp/kites/fak/science/science.html*

Sneider, C.I. 1988. *Height-O-Meters*. Berkeley, CA: Lawrence Hall of Science.

Figure 4
Four-cell tetrahedron

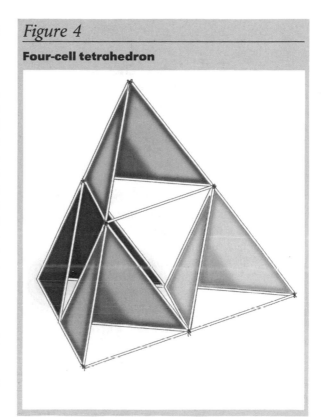

Figure 5
Bridle attachment

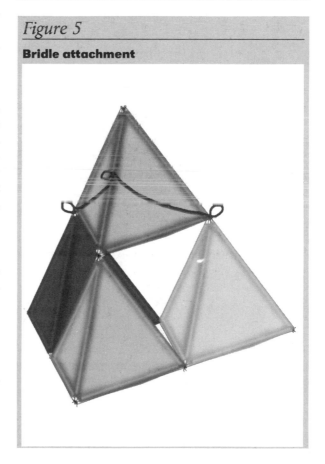

Standards

Science
Understanding Concepts and Processes
- Evidence, models, and explanation

Science as Inquiry
- Abilities necessary to do scientific inquiry
- Understanding about scientific inquiry

Physical Science
- Motion and forces

Science and Technology
- Abilities of technological design
- Understanding about science and technology

ADAPTED FROM *NSES*, TABLE 6.9, P. 110

Math
Important skills that relate to the geometry of kites were drawn from the National Council of Teachers of Mathematics standards. Specific standards that are supported by these activities include the following:

- Analyze characteristics and properties of two- and three-dimensional geometric shapes.
- Specify locations and describe spatial relationships using coordinate geometry and other representational systems.
- Apply transformations and use symmetry to analyze mathematical situations.
- Use visualization, spatial reasoning, and geometric modeling to solve problems.

Sneider, C.I. 1989. *Experimenting with model rockets*. Berkeley, CA: Lawrence Hall of Science.

Resources
Eden, M. 1998. *The magnificent book of kites*. New York: Black Dog and Leventhal.

Hosking, W. 1992. *Kites in the classroom*. Rockville, MD: American Kitefliers Association.

Howe, A. C. 2002. *Engaging children in science*. Upper Saddle River, NJ: Merrill.

Mathison, C., and C. Mason. 1989. Planning interdisciplinary curriculum: A systematic and cooperative approach. Presentation at ASCD Annual Conference, Orlando, FL.

Pelham, D. 1976. *Kites*. Woodstock, NY: Overlook Press.

Internet Resources
Kites Webquest
   http://imet.csus.edu/imet1/richardek/webquest/index.html
A Look at the Mandala as an Art Form
   www.dartmouth.edu/~matc/math5.pattern/lesson1art.html
NCTM Principles and Standards for School Mathematics
   http://standards.nctm.org
Power Kite Site
   www.kitepower.com
Sierpinsky's Tetrahedron
   www.melbpc.org.au/pcupdate/9902/9902article5.htm
Tetrahedron Kites
   http://gw011.k12.sd.us/TetrahedronKites.htm
Wolfram Math World: Tetrahedron
   http://mathworld.wolfram.com/Tetrahedron.html

This article first appeared in the March 2004 issue of Science Scope.

Chapter 4

String Racers

by Bruce Yeany

INSTRUCTIONAL INFORMATION

Overview

String racers are an effective way to demonstrate Newton's third law. This set of instructions gives plans for two types of string racers: the simple balloon racers that are quick and easy to build and a rubber band–powered propeller design that can race down a string 80 ft. or more. Both of these pieces can be built and demonstrated simply as an example of action reaction, or they can be incorporated in a project-building assignment for students to test a variety of design objectives.

Student Skills

Observation. The string racer and the balloon will move forward as a result of air pushed backward.
Design and Construct. Students can build a copy of the string racer with the plans provided, or they can design their own version and try to improve its performance. Other variations of the propeller and tube can be adapted for use on land or water.
Application. Students can look for other examples of propulsion or forward movement as a result of air being pushed backward.

Related Concepts or Processes

Potential energy	Friction
Kinetic energy	Newton's second law
Inertia	Newton's third law
Simple machines	Speed
Design	Testing of hypothesis
Trial and error	Construction techniques

Prior Knowledge

You can use these pieces for early elementary students if you use them as a demonstration. Younger students should be able to define motion. Prior introduction to the application of force as a push or a pull is helpful. They should understand that forces are needed to

---

SAFETY NOTE

The moving propeller can hurt fingers or cut skin if it hits someone while it is spinning. Students must be careful not to let the spinning propeller hit their fingers upon release and must not try to catch the racer before it stops.

The string racer can move quite quickly down the string, possibly jumping off the holder along the way. Instruct students to stand back from the moving string racers.

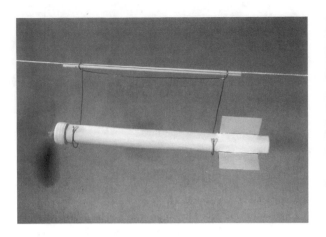
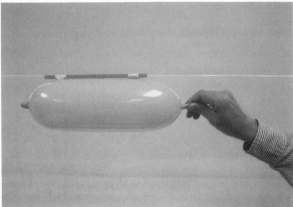

make things move and that friction slows objects down and eventually stops them. Older students should have some basic understanding about motion and how we can measure it. They may have been introduced to some ideas about storing energy versus energy being used. These pieces also can be used to demonstrate Newton's laws of motion.

Predemonstration Discussion

Students can review the ideas of how forces are applied and energy is needed to make objects move through numerous examples. You should demonstrate wind-up toys, lift a ball up and then allow it to roll down a table, and show the balloon racer before introducing the string racer. A number of questions are applicable; use those that apply to the age of your students. Some questions for discussion include the following:

*   What is needed to make an object move?
*   How can we add energy to make things move?
*   What are some ways that toys or objects can store energy?
*   What are some ideas that affect the distance that an object will move?
*   Why do moving objects slow down?

Suggestions for Presentation

Thread a long string through a drinking straw and then tie it so it extends from one end of the room to the other. A successful sequence might start with a demonstration of a deflated balloon and a discussion of how energy can be added to the balloon. After energy is added, students can predict how the balloon will move if it is released. If you have other shapes of balloons, discuss what flight characteristic each might have.

The discussion about the untethered balloon should lead into attaching the balloon to the string. This allows for a more efficient movement. The string

helps stabilize the movement of the balloon and directs the air backward. The balloon is then propelled forward, usually at a higher rate of speed than in the untethered mode, because less energy is lost to extraneous movements.

The propeller-driven string racer can follow the balloon racer. Attach the wire holder to the string. It is easier to wind up this string racer first and then attach it to the holder. Try not to pull down on the string racer as the propeller is released because that will make it bounce up and waste a lot of energy.

Interactive questions about balloon energy could include the following:

*   Does a deflated balloon have any potential energy?
*   How can we put energy into it?
*   What happens if I let the inflated balloon go?
*   Why does it not travel in a straight path?
*   How can we get the balloon to travel in a straight path?

Interactive questions about the balloon racer could include the following:

*   How does the flight characteristic change when the balloon is tethered to the string?
*   Compare the speed of the tethered and the untethered balloons.
*   Why does the tethered balloon move faster?
*   If the balloon goes forward, what must the particles of air do?
*   How would the amount of air put into the balloon affect the speed and distance that it travels?
*   How can we calculate the speed of this racer?

Interactive questions about the propeller-driven racer could include the following:

Figure 1

Typical example of a student-designed string racer

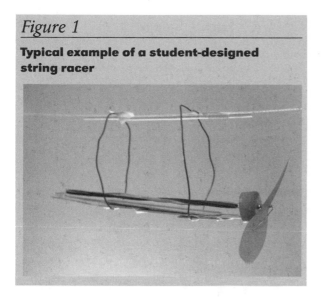

- What are the similarities between the balloon racer and the propeller racer?
- What are the differences between the balloon racer and the propeller racer?
- How does this vehicle move?
- How does a propeller push air backward?
- What are some variables that might change the speed and distance that the racer travels?
- How can we calculate the speed of this vehicle?

Postdemonstration Activities and Discussion

The propeller-driven string racer was originally designed as a building project for elementary students. A pattern was printed on heavy stock paper by using a copying machine. The bottle caps had holes added to them, and students assembled the propeller system. It is a simple project that fourth- and fifth-graders can build with some assistance from an adult. When used as a demonstration for middle school students, this propeller-driven racer generated the same enthusiasm it did among the younger children. Knowing that the purpose of the fins is to keep the string racer from turning as it travels from one end to the other, middle school students found it interesting to use larger fins and adjust them so that the string racer would do two or three loops as it traveled from one end to the other.

Propeller-driven string racers can also be the basis for a design project. Give students a variety of materials, and challenge them to construct a device that will travel down the string as quickly as possible. You can show the string racer as an example of how it can be done, although this usually results in students' copying it and may limit the designs students will try.

Figure 1 is a typical example of a student-designed string racer. In this case, students were not shown any examples before they were given the assignment.

Students tried using the propellers to push or pull the string racer. Both ways can be successful. Most students stuck with a single propeller; some tried using two propellers, and a few tried three. Usually, the simplest designs are the most effective.

Suggested Materials
Purchased propellers or propellers made from tongue depressors, soda bottle caps, soda bottles, cardboard, paper, mat board, 18-gauge steel wire, foam meat trays, paper clips, 8 in. long rubber bands, balsa wood, glue gun, tape, wheels, K'nex, LEGOs.

The string racers can demonstrate several concepts of force and motion. For example, they show potential energy changing into kinetic energy. The balloon racer stores energy (potential) by stretching the latex fabric. This energy changes into kinetic energy by pushing the gases out of the end. The string racer stores energy by twisting the rubber band and uses the propeller to pull the device through the air as it pushes air backward.

String racers can demonstrate Newton's laws of motion. The devices continue traveling forward even after the balloon empties or the rubber band unwinds. This is an example of inertia. Both of these pieces slow down and eventually stop due to friction between the string and the straw. Newton's second law explains the relationship between force, mass, and acceleration. The movement of the racers can demonstrate how an increase of mass can decrease the acceleration. You can also demonstrate Newton's second law by changing the force. The amount of force is determined by how many rubber bands are turning the propeller, so changing the number of rubber bands affects the acceleration. Newton's third law talks about action and reaction. Both of these devices go forward by applying a force backward. In either case, students can feel the air particles being moved backward.

Additional Activities

Have students keep a journal to trace their progress through this problem-solving activity, designing sketches that can be part of the journal and including ideas that worked and those that did not.

Another form of transportation for the propeller-powered tube can be some type of wheeled car. The base supports are carved from foam insulation material. The wheels and axles fit through a plastic drinking straw. The straw is glued into place using a hot glue gun. Rubber bands are used to attach the propeller tube to the supports.

SAFETY NOTE

The moving propeller can hurt fingers or cut skin if it hits someone while it is spinning. Students need to be careful not to let the spinning propeller hit their fingers or skin.

Propeller String Racer

Materials

- 2 sheets of heavy stock paper
- 1 soda bottle cap, any size
- 2 small paper clips
- 1 small plastic bead
- 1 plastic drinking straw
- 3 rubber bands
- 24 in. of thin gauge metal wire
- 1 plastic propeller or tongue depressor for homemade propeller
- Plastic or masking tape
- 50-plus ft. of string
- Scissors
- Large dowel rod
- Ruler
- Sharp-pointed object
- Pliers
- Sandpaper or nail file

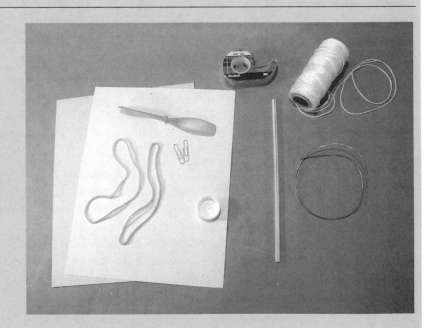

The string racer and variations are all based on the same design using the tube and propeller as the power supply source.

Propeller String Racer

1. To make the tube for the body, start by cutting three slits into the bottom corner of the heavy stock paper. The slits are needed for the fins of the tail section to fit through. Cut the slits 2 in. long and 1 in. apart. Start them ½ in. from the right side edge and ½ in. from the bottom edge. Use a pen to draw thick lines onto the stock paper.

2. You can cut the slits using the edge of the scissors as a cutting edge.

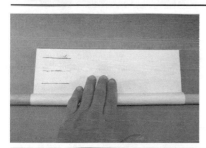

3. After cutting the slits for the fins, roll the paper into a cylinder shape a few times to help retain this shape. Use a large dowel rod as a guide for the rolling process. Make sure the slits appear on the outermost layer of this tube instead of on the inside.

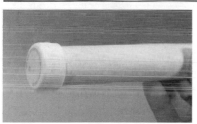

4. The tube will eventually fit snugly in a soda bottle cap. Use the bottle cap to determine the correct size.

5. Make the fins for the tail section from another piece of heavy stock paper. Use a ruler to measure and then draw a pattern that is 2 in. wide and 10 in. long. Use a ruler to measure and then mark off 1 in. blocks for the folding lines. Draw nine lines across the 2 in. width of the tail section.

6. Cut out the 2 in. × 10 in. section with scissors.

chapter 4

7. This pattern is for folding the tail section. Each line indicates where to fold the heavy stock paper.

8. Use a straight edge in the folding process to help ensure the folded lines match the drawn lines. The folds must be accurate to ensure that they match up with the slits cut in the body tube.

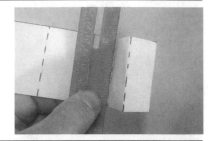

9. The creases in the paper must be well defined. Lay the fold on a hard surface and press and slide the ruler against the fold. Do this with each fold.

10. Fold the tailpieces tightly together. Each tail fin is made from two pieces of the paper folded together. You can cut these fins to resemble a rocket-tail assembly after they are inserted in the tube body.

11. Unroll enough of the body tube so that the folded tabs for the tail section can be inserted into the slots cut into the body tube.

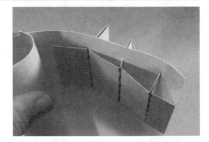

12. Roll the paper and fins back into the cylinder shape again. The fins should be evenly spaced in the back end of the cylinder.

The fins help stabilize the string racer as it moves on the string. They can be adjusted to make the string racer do loops as it travels down the string.

13. The tube diameter should be approximately the same as the inside diameter of the bottle cap. Check the tube diameter at the front and back ends of the tube using the bottle cap.

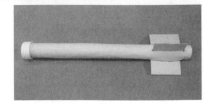

14. Apply a few pieces of tape in the tail section area and along the tube body to keep the tube from unrolling.

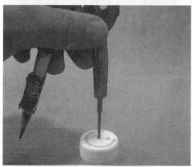

15. To assemble the propeller, start by removing the inner liner from a soda bottle cap and then use a pointed object such as an ice pick or compass to poke a hole through the center. The hole should be just slightly larger than the diameter of the paper clip.

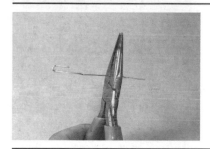

16. Make the shaft for the propeller from a paper clip. Unbend two of the three bends. Leave the smallest of the three bends in place. This shaft should resemble a J. If the paper clip is too long, cut it using the cutting edge of pliers.

17. For a smoother operation, the propeller should turn in a straight path without any wobbles. The area where the shaft goes through the propeller is rounded. Sand the rounded tip of the propeller shaft flat, using a fine-grit sandpaper or nail file.

18. Begin the assembly of the propeller by pushing the straightened end of the paper clip through the hole in the soda cap. The hooked end of the paper clip is toward the inside of the bottle cap. Now add a small bead with flat ends to the paper clip shaft, followed by the propeller. The bead will act as a washer between the cap and propeller and allow it to turn more efficiently.

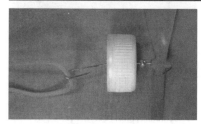

19. Use the pliers to bend over ¼ in. of the paper clip to catch the propeller.

The speed of the racer is dependent on the number of rubber bands used to propel it; three or four usually work very nicely. Hook the rubber bands onto the J portion of the paper-clip shaft. Bend the end of the paper clip over the rubber bands to hold them in place.

20. Hook the other end of the rubber band onto another paper clip. Tie a short string onto this paper clip to ease the fitting of the rubber bands through the body tube.

21. To assemble the propeller onto the body, hold the tube vertically and dangle the string into the tube. After the string comes through the opposite end of the racer body, pull on the string to stretch the rubber bands.

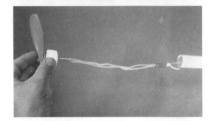

22. To attach the rubber bands to the racer body, hook one of the bends of the paper clip onto the tail section of the tube body.

23. The body of the racer is completed. Wind it up and test it a few times to see how it spins. The propeller should spin without wobbling. If the propeller wobbles, then the paper clip shaft needs some minor adjustments. Do not overwind the rubber bands, or they will break inside the tube.

   The final assembly of the string racer requires that the body be attached to a string that is tied across the room.

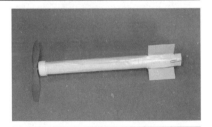

24. A simple method for attaching the racer to the string uses a drinking straw and 24 in. of metal wire. The wire can be bent to hold the racer body to the straw and allow easy attachment or removal of the racer for winding or repairs.

   Start by threading the string through the straw and then tie the string onto two supports.

   Measure and cut off about 24 in. of the wire. The middle 8 in. of the wire remain straight against the straw. Bend the outer sections 90° to form a large *U* section.

25. Bend over the top ½ in. of the 8 in. wire section to clip onto the straw. Use a dowel rod or pencil to form the bend in each corner of the wire. Don't make the bends too tight, or they will pinch the string inside the straw when it is attached.

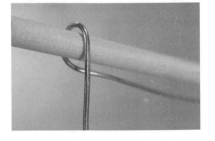

26. Make the second set of bends in the wire hanger about 6 in. down from the straw. Wrap a 1 in. circular bend in the wire around the racer body to hold it in place. The bends must hold the racer enough beneath the straw so that the propeller does not come in contact with the string. Wrap the wire around the racer body for about three-quarters of the distance around. Cut off the excess wire using wire-cutting pliers. The last ¼ in. of the wire should be folded back on itself to form a very small loop that makes a blunt edge.

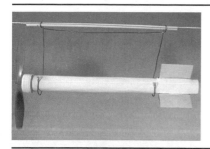

27. The racer body is now ready for a practice run. Wind the rubber bands up by turning the propeller. Place the racer back onto the wire supports while holding the propeller and then let it go.

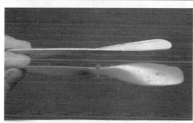

Alternate Propellers

An alternative to purchased propellers is having students make their own. Several designs can be built and tested. Typical purchased propellers have the blades offset by 90°.

1. A tongue depressor can be formed into the same shape as a purchased propeller by twisting it 90° from one end to the other.

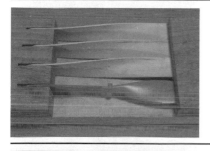

2. If you soak the tongue depressor in water for about an hour, it will become soft and pliable and can be easily bent. A simple form for holding the tongue depressors has four horizontal and four vertical slits about 4 in. apart. Place the wet tongue depressors in this form until they dry. After they dry, they will retain the 90° twist. Then drill a hole in the center for the propeller axle.

Balloon Racer

Materials
- 1 straw
- 1 long thin balloon
- Masking tape
- 50-plus ft. of string

Balloon Racer

1. Thread a string through a drinking straw and tie it to two supports about 20 to 40 ft. apart.

   Wrap a short piece of masking tape with the sticky side out on the front edge of the straw. Wrap another piece of tape with the sticky side out on the other end of the straw.

   Do not wrap the tape too tightly around the straw. Success depends on whether the tape can slide back and forth on the straw with very little effort.

2. To operate this racer, blow up the balloon to its maximum size. While holding the balloon, lift it to the straw and press the center of the balloon onto the sticky sides of the tape.

    Release the balloon when you are ready. The balloon should race down the length of the string.

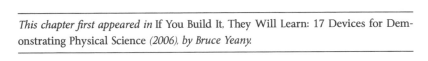

3. A successful trial should have the balloon still on the straw with both tapes moving toward the center of the straw.

This chapter first appeared in If You Build It, They Will Learn: 17 Devices for Demonstrating Physical Science *(2006), by Bruce Yeany.*

Chapter 5

The Tower Challenge

by John Eichinger

OVERVIEW

This activity is an exciting and highly interactive opportunity for students to exercise their creativity and design skills. Working in cooperative groups, students are challenged to explore the geometry of tower design and construction, first by experimenting with possible designs and then by choosing the most likely design candidate and building the tallest tower possible with only paper and tape. This activity is easily connected to social studies via discussion of the world's tall towers or to human anatomy via discussion of the long bones of the body (which act like towers).

PROCESSES/SKILLS

- Observing
- Measuring
- Describing

Further Reading

- "Paper Towers," from the November 2006 issue of *Science Scope*

- Inferring
- Experimenting
- Communicating
- Developing spatial reasoning
- Constructing
- Comparing
- Reflecting
- Recognizing shapes and patterns
- Problem solving

RECOMMENDED FOR

Grades 5–8: Small-group instruction
Adjust for grades 5 and 6 by considering the specific shapes of tall towers in detail during Procedure 1.

TIME REQUIRED

1–2 hours

MATERIALS REQUIRED FOR MAIN ACTIVITY

- Standard 8.5 × 11 inch paper (two different colors)
- Masking tape
- Metersticks
- Scissors

CONNECTING TO THE STANDARDS

NSES
Grade 5–8 Content Standards:
Standard A: Science as Inquiry
- Abilities necessary to do scientific inquiry (especially thinking critically, using evidence, and applying mathematics)
- Understanding about scientific inquiry (especially emphasizing the value of evidence and mathematics)

Standard E: Science and Technology
- Abilities of technological design (especially identifying, implementing, and evaluating a design solution)
- Understanding about science and technology (especially that science and technology work together, and that technological designs have limitations)

NCTM
Standards for Grades 3–8:
- Geometry (especially identifying, naming, comparing, and applying three-dimensional shapes)
- Measurement (especially understanding and applying the metric system)
- Problem Solving (especially applying strategies to solve problems)
- Reasoning and Proof (especially engaging in thinking and reasoning)

SAFETY CONSIDERATIONS

Basic classroom safety practices apply.

ACTIVITY OBJECTIVES

In this activity, students
- successfully design, construct, and evaluate free-standing paper towers;
- measure towers accurately and recognize geometric shapes in their tower designs; and
- compare their paper towers to famous or familiar towers of the world.

MAIN ACTIVITY, STEP-BY-STEP PROCEDURES

1. Brainstorm with students. Start by asking, "What towers have you seen or visited?" Consider famous towers (e.g., Eiffel Tower, Watts Towers, Leaning Tower of Pisa), skyscrapers, radio transmission towers, and natural towers (e.g., Devils Tower in Wyoming). Point out to students that all "towers" are not necessarily architectural; for example, the long bones of the body such as the humerus and the femur are essentially towers, too. Ask, "What do towers have in common? How are they constructed? If you notice different tower 'varieties,' how would you categorize them?" Leave the brainstormed list(s) on the board to prompt speculation, experimentation, and creativity during tower construction. Be sure that students are considering a wide range of geometric options (in terms of the cross-sectional and vertical shapes of their towers) as they evaluate possible designs.

2. Tell students that you are challenging them to build their own towers in class. The challenge is this: Build the tallest free-standing tower possible from a single piece of paper and 30 cm of masking tape.

3. Present the following ground rules:

   - Your group's final tower may contain only those materials (paper and tape) supplied by the teacher.
   - The tower must not be attached at the base to any surface (e.g., desk, floor) and may not lean against any other surface.
   - You will have 30 minutes for official design and construction.
   - Your tower must stand on its own for 10 seconds or longer.
   - The height will be measured from the base to the highest point.
   - You can have your tower "officially" measured as many times as possible within the 30-minute time limit; that is, you can keep adding to it as time permits.

4. The following scoring plan pits students only against gravity and eliminates any overt and unnecessary competition between groups:
   Over 50 cm = Good
   Over 80 cm = Outstanding
   Over 100 cm = Spectacular
   Over 150 cm = A Masterpiece of Engineering and Design!

5. Tower-building time should be broken into two sections: practice time and official time. Practice time lasts for 30 minutes. Student groups receive several pieces of paper, scissors, 30 cm of masking tape, and a meterstick to check their progress. Ask and brainstorm, "What possible shapes or designs could you use?" Students should be encouraged to

test as wide a variety of tower designs as possible to find the one with the greatest potential. For younger students, allow more practice time and be willing to help with design ideas.

Keep in mind that air conditioning, open doors, and open windows can create breezes that will topple towers and frustrate participants during this activity.

6. Official tower time begins when practice period ends and lasts for another 30 minutes. Be sure that students surrender any extra paper and tape left over from practice time. You could take a break between the two periods to discuss practice efforts, likely structural candidates, and so on. This discussion allows students to hypothesize about the tower designs that are most likely to meet the challenge. Or, to encourage separate efforts by the student construction groups, you could dispense with the discussion, moving directly from practice time into official time.

7. When official time begins, student groups receive a single sheet of paper and another 30 cm of tape. To make sure practice paper is not accidentally incorporated into official towers (thus providing extra construction material), use two different colors of paper, one for practice and one for the official tower. With a list of student groups in hand, circulate and verify student tower height measurements whenever students ask, documenting their progress on the list. They may continue to add to their towers throughout the time period, so some groups may ask to be officially measured more than once.

8. Conclude with a classwide discussion and analysis of the activity, including a presentation of each of the towers constructed. Ask students, "What would you do differently next time? What did you enjoy about this activity? What would you like to know about towers?"

DISCUSSION QUESTIONS

Ask students the following.

1. Which designs worked? Which didn't? How do you explain these results?

2. What geometric shapes do you see in the completed towers? (Consider the towers in cross-section as well as in lateral view.) With what other shapes did you experiment? Why do you suppose that certain shapes work better than others in tower design?

3. How important were measurements in this activity? Explain your answer.

Sample Rubric Using These Assessment Options

	Achievement Level		
	Developing 1	Proficient 2	Exemplary 3
Were students actively involved in building and analyzing the design of free standing paper towers?	Only marginally involved with tower design, construction, and analysis	Appropriately and significantly involved in tower design, construction, and analysis	Took a leadership role in tower design, construction, and analysis
Were students able to recognize geometric shapes in their tower designs?	Unsuccessfully attempted to identify geometric shapes in their tower designs	Recognized several geometric shapes in their tower designs	Recognized geometric shapes and could explain their impact on tower design
Were students able to measure accurately?	Unsuccessfully attempted to measure tower height	Successfully measured tower height	Successfully measured several aspects of tower design
Were students able to explain similarities and differences between real towers and their own paper towers?	Unsuccessfully attempted to explain similarities and differences between real towers and their own to any significant extent	Successfully explained several similarities and differences between real towers and their own	Successfully explained similarities and differences and were also able to explain their implications for tower design and construction

4. How did your completed towers compare with the real towers we listed on the chalkboard? How were your towers similar to those? How did they differ?

5. What sort of training do you think a person would need if he or she wanted to design and build real towers?

ASSESSMENT

Suggestions for specific ways to assess student understanding are provided in parentheses.

1. Were students actively involved in building and analyzing the design of free-standing paper towers? (Use observations made during Procedures 5–7 as performance assessments, and use responses to Discussion Question 1 as embedded assessment.)

2. Were students able to recognize geometric shapes in their tower designs? (Use Discussion Question 2 as embedded evidence or as a prompt for a science journal entry.)

3. Were students able to measure accurately? (Use observations made during Procedures 5 and 7 as performance assessments, and use responses to Discussion Question 3 as embedded assessment.)

4. Were students able to explain similarities and differences between real towers and their own paper towers? (Use Discussion Question 4 as embedded evidence or as a prompt for a science journal entry.)

OTHER OPTIONS AND EXTENSIONS

1. Homework: Ask students to identify towers or towerlike structures in their homes or in the community. As a further extension, students can draw the structures or construct three-dimensional models.

2. Instruct students to build a paper model of a real tower (e.g., skyscraper, radio tower, Eiffel Tower, Washington Monument, Egyptian obelisk, Leaning Tower of Pisa). This could be done on an individual basis, by cooperative groups, or by the entire class.

3. Have students conduct research (e.g., library, internet, interviews) into various towers of interest: strange towers, tallest towers, towers in history, most beautiful towers, and so on.

4. Rather than building a tall tower, have students design and construct a beautiful tower, a functional tower, an intimidating tower, or a fantasy tower.

Resources

Adams. B. 2006. London Bridge is falling down. *Science and Children* 43 (8): 49–51.

Junior Engineering Technical Society. 1989. Engineering science in the classroom. *Science and Children* 26 (8): 20–23.

Kamii, C. 2006. Measurement of length: How can we teach it better? *Teaching Children Mathematics* 13 (3): 154–158.

Martin, S., J. Sharp, and L. Zachary. 2004. Thinking engineering. *Science and Children* 41 (4): 18–23.

Pace, G., and C. Larsen. 1992. On design technology. *Science and Children* 29 (5): 12–15, 16.

Scarnati, J. 1996. There go the LEGOs. *Science and Children* 33 (7): 28–30.

Tepper, A. B. 1999. A journey through geometry: Designing a city park. *Teaching Children Mathematics* 5 (6): 348.

Toll, D., and S. Stump. 2007. Characteristics of shapes. *Teaching Children Mathematics* 13 (9): 472–473.

This chapter first appeared in Activities Linking Science With Math, 5–8 *(2009), by John Eichinger.*

PART 2

Teacher-Created Constructions and Repurposed Materials

Chapter 6

Recycling Aluminum Cans in the Lab

Two Inexpensive Inquiry Activities

by Ann Ross and Tillman Kennon

Don't throw away that aluminum can! Don't even place it in the recycling bin. Instead, use it in your next science lab. Aluminum cans may be used to determine how many calories are in a peanut or to make an electroscope. In addition to the economic advantages of using materials such as aluminum cans, there are also pedagogical advantages: Physical phenomena demonstrated with simple, familiar objects may have a more lasting effect than demonstrations using more sophisticated apparatus (Kruglak 1992).

PEANUT CALORIMETRY

Food energy is measured in calories (C), each of which equals one kilocalorie. The gross energy value of a food can be determined by actually burning the food and measuring the chemical energy produced as the food is converted to heat energy.

About 75% of the energy in a peanut comes from peanut oil. By burning a peanut, students can indirectly measure the food energy by directly measuring the chemical energy released as the chemical bonds within the peanut oil break down. Peanut oil is flammable, and peanuts will burn when ignited with a match or lighter (see pp. 32–33 for lab instructions).

STATIC ELECTRICITY

When two different materials come into close contact—for example, wool rubbing against a balloon—electrons may be transferred from the wool to the balloon. When this happens, the area on the balloon that was in contact with the wool ends up with an excess of electrons and becomes negatively charged, while the wool ends up with a shortage of electrons and becomes more positively charged. This buildup of unequal charges on objects is commonly referred to as *static electricity*.

Materials such as the rubber that balloons are constructed of are called *insulators*. Therefore, it is possible for the majority of the surface area of the balloon to remain neutrally charged while the part that was rubbed by the wool becomes negatively charged.

Protons and neutrons are located in the nuclei of atoms and normally do not move. It is important for students to explain their observations in terms of the electrons moving from one object to the next and what the end results are. If an object that has acquired a charge, such as the balloon described above, is moved close to a neutral object, such as a Styrofoam ball, the ball will become positively charged by *induction*. This can be explained by the big rule in electricity and magnetism—likes repel while opposites attract.

The electrophorus lab (see p. 34) demonstrates these concepts by allowing students to see static electricity in action. A pie pan serves as the charged object that induces a charge in a soda can simply by being moved near the bottom of the can (induction). If the charged pie pan touches the soda can, the electrons actually flow into the soda can, charging it by *conduction*. Instruct students to explain their observations in terms of which direction the electrons move, and whether the observed reaction was caused by induction or conduction.

CONCLUSION

Many other demonstrations and experiments can be performed using aluminum cans and other recycled materials. For example, aluminum cans can be used to demonstrate pressure. Students can predict what will happen when a small amount of water is heated to boiling inside a can and the can is quickly inverted in cold water (the can implodes). If the can is not inverted in water, nothing happens. Students can predict whether a diet or regular soda will sink or float (the diet soda will float).

Of course, soda cans aren't the only familiar objects that teachers and students can use for science activities. Eggs can be used to demonstrate inertia (a raw egg will continue to spin after being lightly touched). Cornstarch and water can produce "oobleck," a non-Newtonian type of matter. Straws can be used as musical instruments to illustrate the physics of sound. Milk containers can be used as terrariums. Another benefit of such activities is that by using

---

Peanut Calorimetry Lab (Trautwein and Ross 1999)

Safety Notes
Before performing this lab, you must check with the school nurse or parents regarding student allergies to peanuts or other nuts. This lab should be performed in a well-ventilated classroom, safety glasses must be worn at all times, and students with long hair will need to tie their hair back.

Materials
(Per group of four students)
- Aluminum soda can
- Ring stand with iron ring
- Clay triangle or wire screen
- Balance (electronic, if available, one per class)
- Jumbo paper clip
- Alcohol thermometer or temperature probe
- 100 ml graduated cylinder
- Beaker with water for used match stems
- Safety glasses
- Stirring rod
- Butane lighter
- Peanut or other type of nut, such as almonds, cashews, Brazil nuts, or filberts (Safety note: Nuts may not be eaten!)
- Tweezers (for handling hot nut)

Figure 1

Peanut calorimeter

- Beaker tongs or heat-proof gloves (for handling hot can)
- Hot pad or other heat-resistant surface

Procedure
(See Figure 1 for a photograph of an assembled peanut calorimeter.)
1. Pour 100 g of water into the soda can. (In the metric system, 100 ml of water has a mass of 100 g). (Safety note: Watch for sharp edges on the can.) Support the can on the ring stand by setting it on a clay triangle or wire screen.
2. Measure the mass of one nut, preferably on an electronic balance. Record the mass in the data table.
3. Position the nut on the stand base using a paper clip. (Bend one end of the paper clip so that it rests on the base and make a loop at the other end to support the peanut. Instead of making a loop, you might try opening up the end of the paper clip and pushing it through the nut.) Place the paper clip supporting the nut on the base of the ring stand. Position the soda can about 3 cm over the nut.
4. Measure the temperature of the water before it has been heated using the thermometer or temperature probe. Record the temperature in the data table. Remove the thermometer while the heating is taking place.

Peanut Calorimetry Lab *(Trautwein and Ross 1999)*

5. Wearing safety goggles and with long hair tied back, light the nut with the lighter. The nut will continue to burn after it is ignited.
6. Stir the water gently with the stirring rod as the nut burns. (Inform the teacher if your thermometer is broken.) It will take up to five minutes for the nut to burn completely.
7. When the nut is completely burned, remove the stirring rod and again measure the temperature of the water.
8. Remove the remains of the burned nut with tweezers. You may need to brush the ashes onto a small piece of paper placed near the nut in order to ensure that all of the burned nut is collected. Using the balance, find the mass of the burned nut. Record the mass in the data table.
9. Calculate the change in the mass of the nut and the rise in the temperature of the water.
10. Repeat, using another variety of nut, such as a cashew, Brazil nut, almond, or filbert. Start with cold water each time.
11. Let the can cool before you remove it from the ring stand (or remove the hot can from the ring stand with the beaker tongs and place it on the hot pad).

12. Calculate the number of calories required to produce the observed temperature change by multiplying the change in temperature of the water by the mass of the water (100 g). Divide this number by 1,000 to get the number of kilocalories. (Remember, food energy is measured in calories, which are actually kilocalories.)
13. Divide the kilocalories (C) by the mass of the nut that was burned to get the kilocalories per gram.

Questions for Students
1. Why was the mass of the nut less after it burned?
2. What happened to the energy that was stored in the nut?
3. Was all of the mass of the nut that burned converted into energy? Was some of it "lost"? (Hint: What about the smoke and soot generated?)
4. Did different types of nuts produce different amounts of energy (C/gram)?
5. Are nuts a good source of energy? Are there additives to foods such as peanut butter that add to the number of calories per serving?

Extension
Students could conduct surveys of various food groups to determine the number of calories per gram by reading food labels.

Data Table

	Peanut	Cashew	Almond	Brazil Nut	Filbert
Mass of nut before burning (grams)					
Mass of nut after burning (grams)					
Mass of nut that was burned (grams)					
Temperature change of 100 g of water (degrees Celsius)					
Calories required to produce observed temperature change in the 100 ml of water (equals the calories in the nut) Hint: 1 calorie = heat required to change the temperature of 1 gram of water 1°C					
Kilocalories per gram: Change calories to kilocalories; divide the kilocalories by the mass of nut burned					

Soda-Can Electroscope and Electrophorus Lab (Kruglak 1992)

Note

Static-electricity activities are most successful and exciting on days when there is low relative humidity. When there is a large amount of moisture in the air, some of it forms a coating on the surfaces of objects. This surface coating of moisture can neutralize a buildup of static charge.

Materials

(Per group of four students)

- Aluminum soda can
- Styrofoam coffee cup
- Styrofoam insulation board or other Styrofoam products, such as picnic plates
- Disposable aluminum pie pan
- Wool, fur, or other cloth
- 1 cm × 10 cm aluminum foil
- Masking tape
- Balloons or drinking straws (optional)

Soda-Can Electroscope Procedure

(See Figure 2 for a photograph of an assembled soda-can electroscope and electrophorus apparatus.)

1. Carefully bend the tab-top on the aluminum can so that it sticks straight out from the end of the can. (Safety note: Watch for sharp edges on the can.)
2. Set the Styrofoam cup upside down and tape the soda can horizontally on top of the cup.
3. Roll a 0.5 cm × 3 cm strip of aluminum foil around a drinking straw to form a hook on one end of the strip, and hang the hook over the end of the pull tab.
4. Use your electrophorus apparatus (see instructions below) to charge the electroscope.
5. When the charged object is brought near the can, the foil leaves should repel each other. In addition to the pie-plate electrophorus apparatus, other charged objects could include balloons or vinyl strips such as a drinking straw.

Electrophorus Apparatus Procedure

1. Cut a 30 cm square of Styrofoam insulation for the base or use a Styrofoam picnic plate placed upside down.
2. Fasten an insulating handle to an aluminum pie pan by taping a Styrofoam cup in the center of the pan.

Figure 2

Soda-can electroscope and electrophorus apparatus

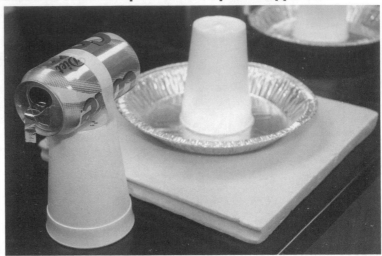

3. To use the electrophorus, rub the top surface of the foam base or plate with fur or cloth to charge it. Then set the pan on top of the foam, touch the pie pan with your finger (this positively charges the top of the pan), remove your finger, and then lift the pan by the handle.
4. Bring the positively charged pie pan into contact (conduction) with the bottom end of your soda-can electroscope.
5. Repeat the above action, but do not touch the pie pan to the can (induction).

Questions for Students

1. Charge a straw by rubbing it on a piece of cloth or through your hair. Position the straw near the foil strips attached on the end of the soda can. Describe what you observe and give an explanation.
2. Bring a positively charged pie plate into contact (conduction) with the bottom end of the can. Describe what you observe and give an explanation.
3. Repeat the above action, but do not touch the pie pan to the can (induction). What happened and why?
4. Using the electrophorus device, charge the pie pan negatively. Explain your observations.
5. Charge the pie pan positively. Explain your observations.

ordinary household items and proper safety precautions, students can demonstrate and explain the same experiments at home that they did at school, which reinforces learning.

These activities can also be used as discrepant events to introduce topics and help dispel misconceptions. For example, blowing across a sheet of paper demonstrates Bernoulli's principle, a pencil in a glass of water appears bent due to refraction, and food coloring appears to move faster through hot water than in cold water due to convection.

Most school budgets are inadequate for science teaching materials. Teachers can find many recycled materials at yard sales to use in the science classroom. They can prepare lists of items that students and parents can collect throughout the year for use in their classrooms.

References

Kruglak, H. 1992. "Canned" physics. *The Physics Teacher* 30 (10): 392–96.

Trautwein, J., and A. Ross. 1999. *A physical science laboratory manual.* Dubuque, IA: Kendall/Hunt.

Resources

LaBrecque, J., and R. Morse. 1992. *Teaching about electrostatics: An AAPT/PTRA-PLUS Workshop Manual.* College Park, MD: American Association of Physics Teachers (AAPT).

National Research Council (NRC). 1996. *National science education standards.* Washington, DC: National Academies Press.

Nissani, M., C. L. Maier, and N. Shifrin. 1994. A guided discovery exercise for introductory physics labs. *The Physics Teacher* 32 (2): 104–7.

This article first appeared in the February 2007 issue of Science Scope.

Chapter 7

Materials Repurposed

Find a Wealth of Free Resources at Your Local Recycling Center

by Orvil L. White and J. Scott Townsend

Few teachers find themselves with the support to purchase all the materials they ideally need to supply their classrooms. Buying one or two simple, ready-made items can put a serious strain on anyone's budget. However, materials for science in the classroom need not be prefabricated or expensive. By looking at the function and purpose of any piece of equipment, a creative teacher can find a suitable replacement for many premade science materials, sometimes from the most unlikely places. This is not to say we advocate the potentially hazardous practice known in some circles as "Dumpster diving," but with proper caution and common sense—like partnering with your county's local recycling center—you can find some terrific, serviceable materials among what others have deemed "trash."

Our local recycling center offered a community outreach program called "Materials for the Arts," in which public and homeschool teachers in the county had access to a wealth of materials salvaged from or donated to the recycling center. The center dedicated two rooms at the facility to the program, which stored objects such as clean, sanitized containers of all sizes, including plastic and glass bottles, coffee cans, potato chip cans, baby food jars, and cereal boxes and oatmeal containers; as well as cardboard tubes, carpet squares, compact discs, plastic trays, corkboard, bubble wrap, and other things. All of the materials were required to be completely cleaned with, depending on the material, either antibacterial soap or Lysol spray, before being accepted for donation. Use salvaged materials only if they have been thoroughly sanitized.

If there is no such program in your area, you might consider starting one at your school. Local recycling centers are often looking for outreach opportunities. When we conducted a presentation at our state science teachers' conference a few years ago, several outreach personnel from various state recycling centers approached us for ideas about how they could perform the same outreach services to teachers and the community.

Sometimes we visited the recycling center with specific material needs in mind. Other times, though, we simply explored the rooms to see what ideas were sparked by the materials at hand. Of course, not every item at the recycling center can be repurposed into a useful tool for the science classroom, but here we share a few of our favorites.

TIMER

Teachers can make a classroom timer from two plastic drink bottles with caps and an old 35mm film canister with the bottom removed. Glue the bottle tops together inside the film canister with the tops touching. Trim off the excess canister with kitchen shears, and using an electric drill with a 3/16 bit, drill a small hole through both caps. Place approximately 800 g (for a five-minute timer) of sand, salt, or sugar into one bottle and screw the cap in place. Next, invert the second bottle and screw it into its cap. Test it out and adjust the amount of material as necessary for the time desired. This timer can now be used in a variety of ways, including as a guided-inquiry activity model for students to create other timers of various durations. The timer itself can be used to time speakers, give "time remaining" for a quiz or other assessment, and allow students to better understand the ways in which time has been historically measured.

Using different models of timers, students can investigate questions such as the following: Is there a difference in using sand, sugar, or salt? How does the size (diameter) of the hole in the caps affect the rate at which the materials flow? How does the particle size affect the time it takes for the grains to go through the opening? If using a material other than sand, does the flow rate change over time, and if so, is it faster or slower? Upper elementary or middle school students could also create a graph to show the relationship between mass (in grams) of granular material versus the amount of time it takes for the material to completely travel through the container. This would ultimately allow students to predict how much material they would need to insert for resulting amounts of time in the timer.

SEDIMENT TUBES

Any plastic tube or bottle can be used to show the sedimentation of materials through a water column. We used plastic tubes made from a fluorescent lightbulb cover, a plastic sheath you can buy to cover the bulb, which we cut to size using kitchen shears. The covers are available at most home center outlets. Pour sand or soil into the bottle and fill with water. Know the source of the soil to avoid contaminants. Make sure children wash hands thoroughly after handling soil. Shake and allow the material to settle. The students can observe the soil settling into layers based on the density of the materials contained in the soil.

The sediment tube allows students to model and observe the process of deposition of materials in the natural environment. This process is the prelude to the formation of sedimentary rocks in the Earth's crust. The process of deposition of materials can be used to show how, over geologic time, rocks with differing colors of strata are formed. Students can also

Figure 1

Air circulation demonstration setup

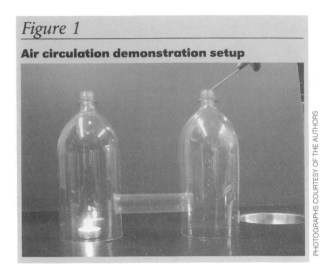

PHOTOGRAPHS COURTESY OF THE AUTHORS

use this method to separate different soils into parts according to grain size and, by measuring the thickness of the layers, calculate percentage of each part—thereby adding a link to mathematics standards. Also, sediment contamination of streams and rivers is an issue in environmental science that can be better visualized and understood once the students can see how soil breaks down and is deposited when mixed with moving water.

DEMONSTRATING CIRCULATION

Recycled materials can also be repurposed for a teacher demonstration exploring air circulation behavior. Remove the bottoms of two 2 L plastic bottles and connect them with a plastic tube, actually a fluorescent lightbulb cover that was cut to size with kitchen shears. Place a small candle under one bottle and hold a lighted stick of incense over the other (see Figure 1). Do this as a teacher demonstration only. Use a tea candle and keep matches out of reach of children. The heated air should rise from the top of the bottle and produce a low-pressure area, drawing the air from the higher-pressure area of the other bottle. This will cause the smoke from the incense to flow down, flow across, and rise with the heated air out of the top, demonstrating the process of air flow in weather systems.

The demonstration models the movement of air in the environment. Air that has been warmed rises, and cold or cooler air moves in to take the place of the warm air. When used as part of a unit on weather, this demonstration enables students to see a process that is generally unobservable and helps explain the shifting wind patterns they can feel. It is useful in exploring sea, land, mountain, and valley breezes, as well as the displacement of warm air when a cold front moves across the landscape. Additionally, this is a good model of how other fluids react when heated. Ocean currents and the movement in a pot of boiling water are other concepts linked to thermal circulation.

GRADUATED CYLINDER AND SCOOPS

You can make a graduated cylinder by measuring a known volume of water into an old plastic bottle, with the label and bottom removed, and marking the measurement with a permanent marker. A clear 1 L water bottle works best for larger volumes, and any smaller straight-sided bottle will work with lesser amounts.

Cutting the bottom of a 1 L bottle will create a scoop that is easy both to use and to pour material from. Scoops can also be made from old salad-dressing bottles cut along the bottom and side. The caps should be glued in place to prevent accidental spills.

FUNNEL AND CUP

A simple funnel can be made by cutting the top off a 2 L bottle and inverting it so the small opening is at the bottom. Aside from their usual use, funnels can be used as part of an inquiry challenging students to design the "most effective" water filtration device. Give students a choice of materials (e.g., coffee filters, paper towels, sand, activated charcoal, shelf liner [the puffy, nonslip type], gravel, cotton balls, sponges, and so on) to design a three-layered water filter within the plastic funnel to remove a small scoop of potting soil from a water sample. Follow all safety rules when working with soil. Know the source of the soil to avoid contaminants and wash hands thoroughly with soap and water after working with soil. The goal for the student groups is to design a filtration system that will result in "clear" water being produced in a timely manner. This activity can be used as a stand-alone inquiry or as part of a larger unit on soils/Earth materials, water quality, or mixtures and solutions and the separation of their component parts.

MYSTERY BOXES

Mystery boxes are a favorite tool for teachers to introduce the meaning of observation and inference and various aspects of the nature of science. Often they are made by purchasing small cardboard boxes from the local jewelry store and placing common classroom or household items in them so students can shake and listen as they try to conclude what is hidden inside. Our local recycling center had a large supply of small cardboard boxes that had once

contained hand soap—voila! We found an ample supply of free mystery boxes! Mystery boxes work well as beginning-of-the-year activities. Using the box, students should first make observations—things they hear or feel. Then they can make an inference—based on the observations, what do you think the object is? Is there any way to know for sure without opening the box? How is this like what a scientist does? This process can help students begin to understand something of the nature of science and what it means to be a scientist.

HOVERCRAFT

Our local recycling center always carries a steady supply of CDs and closable water-bottle tops of different varieties—these materials can be used to make inexpensive hovercrafts. Teachers should build the hovercrafts before presenting them to students for exploration. Using a hot glue gun, teachers glue the base of a water-bottle top that has been cleaned with rubbing alcohol to the center of an old CD (we use the type of spout

Figure 2

A hovercraft

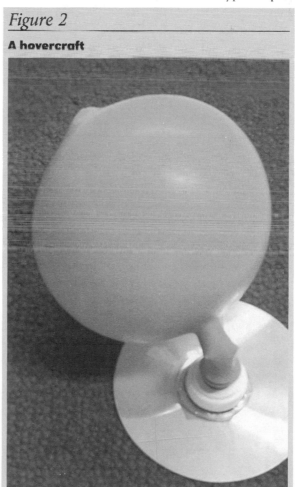

that pulls up to open and pushes down to close because balloons fit easily over these spouts). When the glue is dry, it is ready for use.

To operate the hovercraft, students place an inflated balloon over the closed water-bottle top. When the student pulls up on the bottle top, air from the balloon begins rushing out, causing the craft to move.

We've used these models to introduce such concepts as Newton's laws of motion, friction, and force. For example, before the top is pulled up (and opened), we have the students try pushing their devices across the tables. They note how far each device travels without the air rushing through the top and under the CD. We then have the students pull open the top and try the same process. They quickly observe how much farther the device travels when a force—in this case a push—is applied. We then give the students the option to add washers or other weights to see what happens to the distance the hovercraft travels when the same amount of force (once again a push) is applied. This exploration leads easily to discussion about Newton's laws of motion.

To extend learning beyond exploration with the simple hovercraft, we often challenge students to find ways to make the hovercraft travel without the students pushing it, or we challenge the students to design a hovercraft that will travel farthest when set in front of a fan in the hallway.

These are just a few of the recyclable items we have adapted for use in our classrooms. We

Connecting to the Standards

This article relates to the following *National Science Education Standards* (NRC 1996).

Teaching Standards
Standard A:
Teachers of science plan an inquiry-based science program for their students.

Standard B:
Teachers of science guide and facilitate learning.

Standard D:
Teachers of science design and manage learning environments that provide students with the time, space, and resources needed for learning science.

encourage our fellow teachers to visit their local recycling centers to see what types of reusable science teaching treasures they may find. After all, the only thing better than an effective science teaching tool is a FREE science teaching tool!

Reference

National Research Council (NRC). 1996. *National science education standards.* Washington, DC: National Academies Press.

This article first appeared in the Summer 2008 issue of Science and Children.

Chapter 8

Frugal Equipment Substitutions

A Quick Guide

by Erin Peters

In 15 years, I have had science teaching experiences around the country in rural, suburban, and urban schools. In my travels, I have come across some amazingly clever, economical substitutions for hands-on activities in my physical science classes.

Before any substitutions are made, be sure to check with your district science safety officer that they comply with safety standards for your school. The materials can be purchased at most all-purpose stores. Be sure to make your purchases with funds from the science department budget following all reimbursement procedures for your school. Before soliciting any free materials from businesses in your area, it might be a good idea to get the approval of the science supervisor or principal. I hope that the list below will help those on a shoestring budget provide more hands-on activities for their students.

If You Don't Have . . . Try This!

General classroom materials	
Flexible tape measure	Mark string or yarn • Use one color permanent marker to mark every meter and another color to indicate each centimeter.
Miniature whiteboards	Use Formica sheets • The local hardware store usually sells large sheets of Formica or whiteboard material. • Have them cut the boards into the required size. • Many stores will cut for free if you tell them it is for an educational purpose.
Classroom demonstration balance	Use a large paper clip, tape, and a meterstick • Open the paper clip to look like an *s* and tape the bottom half of the *s* on the 50 cm mark of the meterstick. • If the meterstick is not balanced, attach small bits of clay underneath each side of the meterstick to balance the weight.

If You Don't Have . . . Try This!

Ink for fingerprinting	Use a pencil and tape • Take a fingerprint from a pencil rubbing and preserve it on tape.
Large numbers of "throwaway" items	Find a willing business to contribute • If you need corks, go to your local wine store. • Put your name, contact information, and date of pickup on a bag that is large enough for the items you need, and ask the business owner to put the items in your bag instead of throwing them away. • Pick the bag up promptly and make sure none of the items are contaminated or soiled.
Physics equipment	
Spring scale to measure force	Use two paper clips and a rubber band • Slip the rubber band into the two paper clips so you can pull the rubber band by holding the clips only. • Measure the stretch of the rubber band in centimeters. • If you want to find out how much the rubber band stretches for each Newton, hook one paper clip to a ring stand and hook a 1 kg mass to the bottom paper clip; measure in centimeters and subtract the resting length of the rubber band. • Remember that different rubber bands have different amounts of stretch.
Inclined planes	Use metersticks and tape • Tape metersticks together side by side until you have a ramp of the correct width. • Use textbooks to prop ramps up.
Tracks for small cars	Use garden edging • The black edging that is about 10 cm deep works well.
Pulley	Use a dowel rod or pencil • Wrap the string around the dowel rod as you would the pulley.
Electrical wire	Use tin foil • Cut the tin foil into thin strips to act as wire. • Insulate the "wire" with clear plastic tape.
Chemistry equipment	
Phenolphthalein	Use Ex-Lax • Crush up a tablet and dissolve it in 250 ml of isopropyl alcohol.
Spot plate	Make a transparency • Type 12 *Os* in 72-point font on a sheet of paper. • Spread them out in a 3 x 4 matrix. • Copy them onto a transparency film. • If you have black table tops, you can use a white sheet of paper behind them for maximum visibility.
Pipettes	Use cut-up straws or coffee stirrers • Place the small straw or coffee stirrer into the liquid to be drawn up. • Stop up the open end with your finger. • Release your finger to release the liquid.

This article first appeared in the February 2007 issue of Science Scope.

Chapter 9

Making the Most of Limited Lab Facilities

by Sandy Buczynski

I've taught science in every school location imaginable; often these spaces would be considered less-than-adequate lab facilities. However, regardless of my classroom location, I've been able to come up with creative ways to provide my students with quality, lab-based activities.

The specific strategies I'd like to review are the use of basket labs, progressive hand-rinsing stations, microscaling, manipulatives, and technology. However, before I get started, I want to emphasize that no lab activities can be conducted in a space that hasn't been inspected and approved by those responsible for the safety of facilities in your school district. This may be the local fire marshal or a safety supervisor hired by the district. In particular, you should keep in mind that no lab activities that require safety glasses, open flames, or chemicals can be done in a room that is not properly ventilated and equipped with safety glasses (and sterilizing capabilities) and an appropriate eyewash system. Chemicals also require the presence of a combination acid/flammables cabinet. Do not order chemicals for particular experiments if they cannot be safely stored. When cutting corners, keep safety a priority. If a teacher has to make a choice between safety and hands-on science, safety should be the first consideration in all cases. Finally, if you want to try any of the strategies suggested in this article, please run them by the proper authorities for approval.

WATER

Let's begin with a dry lab space, better known as an ordinary classroom. I have found that rolling coolers make wonderful sinks. When the cooler fills with water, simply roll it into a bathroom with a central drainage opening and unplug the stopper from the bottom of the cooler. The cooler can do double duty as a water table for conducting density experiments, such as comparing the density of a regular can of soda to a can of diet soda, or for surface area experiments, such as building an aluminum foil boat that will float. A large water container is also useful for washing any labware used during the day.

To facilitate hand washing, I place several flat, plastic dish containers of clean water near the exit of the classroom. A pump bottle of hand washing soap near the first container provides the initial wash and then two or three more containers of water provide progressive rinses that allow students to proceed to their next class with clean hands.

If you are in a dry lab space and want to do a lab that requires an eyewash station, you can purchase one with a self-contained water supply for about $300 from science suppliers. If you have a sink in your room, you can also purchase a kit that attaches to the faucet for creating an eyewash station. Before investing in either of these options, check with your science safety director to make sure such devices meet all school safety requirements. Eyewash stations are required to provide an uninterrupted 15-minute flow of water at three gallons per minute.

HEATING ALTERNATIVES

In a lab space with no gas jets for Bunsen burners, consider heating alternatives. An electric "hot pot" that is used to heat water for coffee or tea (approximately $15) can be used as a quick way to provide hot water for an experiment. A microwave oven can be used to melt a jar of agar to pour into Petri dishes, or to heat water or other materials. Single electric burners (approximately $20) can be used in place of hot plates for heating materials in heat-resistant containers. Power strips can be used to increase the electric potential of your classroom, but keep in mind the capacity of the circuit breaker. Circuit breakers are designed to trip or "blow," stopping the flow of electrical current when the designated amperage is exceeded. For example, a 20-ampere fuse should blow when the current through it exceeds 20 amps. Be sure to check this capacity of the circuit so you don't overtax the system and create a fire hazard.

BASKET LABS

Organization is the key to conducting labs in non-lab environments that have been properly equipped for safety. I keep everything needed for a particular experiment or activity in small plastic baskets that are labeled. These are stored on shelves or in cupboards and easily accessed for the lab period (see Figure 1). (Safety caution: Do not store chemicals or perishables in the baskets. Instead, place a card in the basket indicating which chemical or other materials need to be retrieved from the acid/flammables cabinet or other storage area.) Basket labs can be quickly moved from shelf to cart, and then wheeled to a room for immediate use.

For example, for a demonstration of the interaction between soap and fat molecules, my basket would contain a film canister of dishwashing liquid, vials of food coloring, toothpicks, small plastic bowls, and a note to provide fresh skim milk and whole milk. This basket would also include guidance for the inquiry activity. Lab groups would also be provided with safety glasses and two dishes—one with a small amount of

Figure 1

Basket cupboard

CHRISTINE GOESSLING

room-temperature whole milk and the other with skim milk. In this lab, a drop of food coloring is placed in each dish. Special care is taken not to disturb the surface of the milk. A clean toothpick is dipped into the milk dishes and observations made. Then a toothpick dipped in dishwashing detergent is poked into the milk and immediately withdrawn. Predictions and discussion concerning the reaction occurring in the bowl take place. This lab can be done on regular desktops and the used milk collected in a wide-mouth container for disposal at the conclusion of the experiment. See Internet Resources for a cool "surfing scientist" variation of this basket activity.

INTERACTIVE BULLETIN BOARDS

A classroom with few or no materials can benefit greatly from bright and colorful, interactive bulletin boards that double as teaching aids. The study of genetics, for example, can be enhanced with a felt bulletin board displaying black and brown felt mice that adhere to the board and that can be easily rearranged. Under each mouse, letters and question marks are placed that represent a particular gene combination for a monohybrid cross (see Figure 2 for an example). The letters and mouse colors can be changed daily to keep student interest high. See Internet Resources for more engaging interactive bulletin board ideas.

When studying the animal kingdom, another interactive bulletin board idea is to put pictures of animals cut from magazines on one side of the board and animal phyla names on the other. A piece of yarn, attached with a pushpin to a particular animal, provides a matching line for students to pair that animal with its appropriate phylum.

MICROSCALE

Microscaling involves conducting experiments using a smaller quantity and size of materials to provide benefits that include reduced chemical waste, improved lab safety due to decreasing potential exposure to chemicals, reduced costs for chemical purchase and disposal, and decreased storage space necessary for chemicals. However, microscale labs still require all the safety precautions of their full-size counterparts. The microscaling of experiments also encourages students to think about waste minimization.

An example of a lab that can be easily microscaled is the standard acid-base indicator lab. For this lab, create a blackline master of an observation grid and place it inside a plastic sheet protector. Students wearing chemical-splash goggles can observe how acids and bases react with various indicators. To do this, students place one drop of known chemicals from pipettes for pH 1–13 on the sheet protector in the appropriate squares. Then add one drop of the named indicator to each square (see Figure 3). Students make observations on a separate piece of paper. After observing the reaction of known pH samples, chemicals of an unknown pH can be tested in the same manner. To clean up, simply wipe the plastic sheet with a damp paper towel and dispose of the towel. *Safety caution:* An approved eyewash station must be installed in the room.

MODELS

Of course, when you do not have access to the real thing, models provide a nice alternative. Student-constructed models not only provide the learner with an opportunity to study a content area in depth, but also allow a means for sharing that knowledge with the whole class. Beyond traditional tabletop models of atoms and the solar system, today's tech-savvy students can create their own video productions that explore the stages of mitosis and other phenomena.

TECHNOLOGY

Whether you are in a one-computer classroom or have access to a resource lab, there are many virtual labs available today that provide students with an enjoyable solo or group experience. Some of my favorite online lab sites include:

- ScienceCourseware.Org—*www.sciencecourseware.org* Use the free trial to conduct virtual fly, pedigree, leaf, and cardio labs.

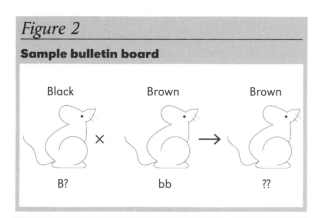

Figure 2

Sample bulletin board

Black × Brown → Brown

B?   bb   ??

Figure 3

pH Indicator	1	3	5	7	9	11	13
Phenolphthalein							
Universal indicator							
Cabbage juice							
Unknown #1							
Unknown #2							
Unknown #3							

- DNA Workshop—*www.pbs.org/wgbh/aso/tryit/dna* Explore transcription and translation.
- Create a DNA Fingerprint—*www.pbs.org/wgbh/nova/sheppard/analyze.html*
- Control of the Cell Cycle—*http://nobelprize.org/educational_games/medicine/2001/cellcycle.html* Simulate mitosis.

Creating learning environments that enable students to engage in science can be accomplished whether the physical facilities cooperate or not—as long as safety concerns are addressed.

ACKNOWLEDGMENT

Special *mahalo* to my colleague Christine Goessling.

Internet Resources
Interactive Bulletin Boards
  http://faculty.kutztown.edu/schaeffe/BulletinBoards/bbs.html
Bread Clip Speedboat
  http://www.abc.net.au/science/surfingscientist/breadclip.htm

This article first appeared in the February 2007 issue of Science Scope.

The FRVGAL Science Teacher

chapter 9

Chapter 10
Balloon in a Bottle

by Bruce Yeany

INSTRUCTIONAL INFORMATION

Overview

Blowing up a balloon inside a bottle is difficult if there is no place for the air to be displaced. Once a balloon is blown up inside the bottle, the balloon remains blown up even with the mouth of the balloon wide open. This project is a handy way to recycle a few soda bottles or juice containers and at the same time investigate air pressure and fluids displacement.

Student Skills

Application. Students should be able to identify other situations in which air pressure is added to closed containers such as tires, an air mattress, or a basketball.

Measurements. Students can try using an air pump or pressure gauge and measure the amount of force exerted by the air inside a tire or ball.

Communication. Students can express their understanding to others through drawings and written explanations.

Related Concepts or Processes

Air pressure	Forces
Compression	Gases
Equilibrium	Vacuum
Closed system	Pressure differential

Prior Knowledge

This demonstration can be used for elementary students if they have a basis of understanding for some simple concepts about matter. To start, students need to know that matter can be found as solids, liquids, and gases. All matter can be changed into any of these three states by adding or removing energy. Gases are particles of matter in constant motion. Gas pressure is the result of particles bouncing off any surface with which they come into contact. Gas pressure can increase or decrease by changing a few variables.

Predemonstration Discussion

Because students already have some ideas about air pressure, a balloon can be a very useful tool for reviewing some of these concepts.

Students can make quick drawings to model what they believe is expressed in the questions that are presented. For example, they can draw a model of the air particles inside and outside a deflated balloon.

After blowing some air into the balloon, ask students to make another drawing to represent a model of how they think the air and balloon have been changed. This picture represents one student's idea. She is showing that the particles inside the balloon are denser than outside the balloon. She was able to express

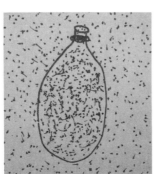

in her writing that the stretched balloon presses the particles closer together. The pressure inside must be greater than outside of the balloon.

Some suggested questions before showing the bottle can include the following:

- Do you think that air pressure is the same throughout this room?
- Why would air pressure balance itself throughout a room?
- What are some factors that can influence that amount of air pressure?
- If we have an empty balloon and its mouth is open, will there be any difference between the pressure inside and outside?
- If we blow up the balloon, what happens inside in terms of air particles?

- If we squeeze the balloon in our hands, what effect does this have on the volume?
- If we change the volume of the balloon, what effect does this have on the particles?
- Why is air added to a soccer ball?

Suggestions for Presentation

Your students can have fun trying the bottle for themselves. Have several extra balloons available. Before adding the balloon to the top of the jar, discuss what is inside. Next fit a balloon into the jar and stretch the mouth over the mouth of the bottle. Screw the soda bottle cap into place to make the bottle airtight. Then ask a student to try to blow up the balloon inside of the jar. Discussion should follow on why this cannot be done. By this time, most students will have noticed the added soda bottle cap. Usually some suggest trying it again without the cap. If the cap is taken off the bottle, the balloon can then be blown up inside. With the balloon blown up, quickly screw the cap back on. The balloon will remain blown up inside the bottle.

It is unusual that a balloon is blown up due to a decrease in pressure on the outside rather than through the normal method of increased pressure on the inside. Students can look through the opening of the mouth and see down into the center of the balloon.

Interactive questions during the presentation could include the following:

- What is inside the jar?
- Is anything truly empty?
- After a balloon is pushed into the jar and then stretched across the mouth, is there still air inside?
- Why is it impossible to blow up the balloon inside the jar?
- Why does removing the little cap allow us to blow up the balloon?
- Why does the balloon stay inflated if the cap is screwed back on?
- What would happen if we unscrew the little cap?
- What is a method for blowing up the balloon inside the bottle without actually touching it?

Postdemonstration Activities and Discussion

- Write and discuss what would happen to the balloon if this demonstration sits for one or two days.
- What would be the results if we run hot water over the bottle?

SAFETY NOTE
Follow normal rules of good hygiene and do not allow more than one person to put his or her mouth on a given balloon or bottle. Prepare extra bottles if necessary.

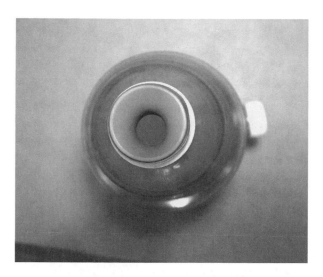

- What would happen if we put the device in the freezer for a few minutes? Try it and then discuss the results.
- What would happen if water is added to the inside of the balloon and then the small cap is removed?
- What would happen if water is added to the inside of the balloon and then the device is allowed to sit for a few days?
- You can construct more than one bottle to show variations in demonstrations.

Try using a long balloon inside the soda bottle instead of a round balloon. If the round balloon is blown up inside the soda bottle, the bottle will deform after you stop blowing and the small cap is screwed into place.

You can ask students why the round balloon deforms the bottle while the long balloon does not.

- Which balloon creates a greater pressure change in the space between the balloon and the bottle?
- What size balloon creates more pressure inside, large or small? Hint: When is it hardest to blow up a balloon, when it is small or as it gets bigger?

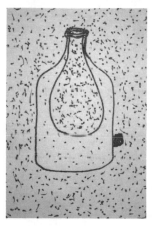

- Have students draw models to explain the results of the suggested changes to the bottle. (This picture represents one student's idea. She is suggesting that the air pressure is decreased inside the bottle but not inside the balloon.)
- Demonstrate the similarities of adding air to other objects such as a soccer ball or a bike tire. A pump with a gauge can help with a discussion on how pressure is measured.
- Have students research the mechanics of the lungs. How do our lungs work? If we want to pull air into our lungs, what does the body do to the lungs? What happens when we exhale?
- Have students make a list of as many objects as possible that have air added to increase the pressure.

Discussion of Results

The amount of pressure is the result of several factors. One factor that pressure depends on is the number of available particles in the gas. Pressure also depends on how frequently and how hard the particles are hitting a surface; this is identified as its kinetic energy. For a given amount of a gas, the volume or size of the container determines or influences the amount of pressure inside. When the amount of gas remains constant and the volume of available space increases, the spacing between the particles increases and the pressure decreases. Decreasing the size of the container has the opposite effect, causing an increase in pressure. Air is a combination of several gases. It exerts pressure against every surface that it touches. Typically, air can exert about 14.7 pounds per square inch of pressure on every surface.

This experiment demonstrates air pressure within a container. As long as air can move into the opening of a container, the pressure will be the same on both the inside and outside. Sealing the mouth of the bottle creates a closed container. When a person tries to blow up a balloon inside the container, he or she is making the available space smaller inside the jar. As the space becomes smaller, the particles are pushed closer together, causing them to collide more frequently and increasing the pressure. The balloon will inflate only a small amount because a person's lungs are not strong enough to compress the air much further.

Next, remove the little soda cap and blow up the balloon inside the bottle. Some of the air particles are pushed out of the soda bottle mouth as the balloon inflates. When the soda cap is placed back on, the balloon stays inflated. The reason is that air is unable to return back into this region. As the balloon tries to deflate, it causes an increase in the volume of space between the balloon and the bottle. As the volume increases, the air pressure drops in this region. Without a passage for the air to get past the balloon into the inner part of the bottle, the balloon membrane will remain stretched. Air from outside the bottle is pushing to get into the area of lower pressure inside the bottle.

One postdemonstration has a student blow up the balloon inside the bottle. The condition is that he or she is not allowed to blow into the balloon. The trick to accomplishing this feat is "sucking" on the soda bottle mouth. By doing so, a person decreases the number of air particles in the region, thus lowering the air pressure. Air pressure outside the bottle inflates the balloon by trying to push into the region. The air is simply trying to equalize itself on both sides of the balloon membrane.

If a 2 L bottle device is constructed, you can use a long balloon inside a 2 L soda bottle to keep it from deforming when attempting the first demonstration. However, a long balloon can also deform the bottle if the balloon is not inflated to its full size.

When a round balloon is used inside a soda bottle, it exerts a greater pressure and causes the bottle walls to collapse. Why does this happen? A long balloon conforms to the shape of the soda bottle much better than a round balloon. It can be blown up more completely and forms a larger size balloon inside the bottle. The amount of pressure exerted by the balloon surface is greater in smaller balloons than in larger balloons. This is exhibited when someone is trying to blow up a balloon. Notice that blowing up a balloon is hard when the balloon is very small but gets easier as the balloon gets larger. Pressure is inversely proportional to the radius of the balloon size, so a small balloon collapses or deforms the bottle wall while a larger balloon does not.

Additional Activities

Many demonstrations show the effects of air pressure against a surface. You can make a simple, easy device from a 10 × 12 in. sheet of rubber, a ½ in. dowel, a wood screw, and a 1 in. fender washer.

The screw and washer are on the bottom side of the rubber sheet. The screw is anchored up into the dowel.

As the rubber sheet is pulled upward, a small space is formed right below the dowel. Because there is no air in this space, it is a vacuum. Outside air is pressing to get into this space. As the air is pressing against the rubber, it holds the table surface and the rubber sheet together.

Set the rubber sheet down against the surface of a desk or table. When someone tries to lift the rubber and dowel upward, he or she will lift the table also.

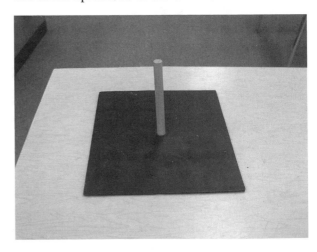

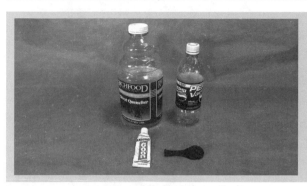

Materials

- 1 plastic bottle, size depends on preference—2 qt., 1 gal., or 2 L
- 1 plastic soda bottle and cap
- 1 large latex balloon
- Silicone glue
- WD-40

Juice bottles are more suitable than the 2 L soda bottle. The juice bottles are made with a heavier gauge plastic and do not deform like the soda bottles.

1. To start, thoroughly clean out both bottles. Remove the label from the 2 qt. juice bottle. To do so, blow air from a hair dryer over the outside of the bottle to loosen the glue and then slowly peel the label off. You can remove the excess glue on the bottle by rubbing it with a solvent or WD-40 lubricant.

2. Use a saw to cut off the top of the soda bottle. Keep a ¼ in. portion of the bottleneck right below the grip ring for gluing this section into the quart bottle.

3. The cut edge of the soda bottle must be smooth; otherwise it will puncture the balloon if the two come in contact. Use sandpaper to smooth the edge of the cut soda bottle top.

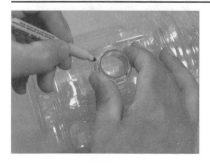

4. Position the soda bottle cap toward the bottom of the bottle, in an area where the bottle is flattened out if possible. Use a pen to trace around the soda bottleneck onto the quart juice bottle.

SAFETY NOTE
Wear work gloves while performing this activity.

The next step is to somehow cut out the area traced onto the bottle. Drilling through the plastic often results in splitting the edges, rendering it useless.

5. The best method of cutting out the correct size hole is to heat a small screwdriver over a stove burner and melt the circumference of the circle. When pushing through the plastic, a sawing action is helpful. Reheat the screwdriver as necessary.

    Check the size of the hole by trying to insert the bottom lip of the soda bottle into this newly cut hole. It should be a snug fit.

6. Firmly glue the soda bottle cap to the plastic bottle. Start by applying a generous bead of glue around the perimeter of the hole.

7. Apply glue also to the bottom edge of the soda bottle lip. Insert the lip into the hole made into the bottle.

8. With the soda bottle top in place, apply more glue around the junction if needed.

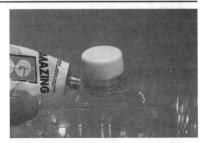

9. Give the glue a few days to dry. The final procedure is to push a large balloon into the mouth of the bottle. Then stretch the opening of the balloon over the mouth of the bottle and fold it downward to keep it in place.

    Caution: Do not twist the bottle cap on too tightly or it may break the glued seal between the bottle and the bottle top.

    The 1 L and 2 L soda bottles, the 1 gal. juice bottle, and a 2 qt. juice bottle are shown ready to go.

    The 2 L soda bottle walls are not as structurally strong as the juice containers. If you used a soda bottle, use long balloons instead of round balloons. The long balloons fit better in the bottle, and they do not deform the bottle when the balloons are left inflated inside the bottle.

This chapter first appeared in If You Build It, They Will Learn *(2006), by Bruce Yeany.*

Chapter 11

Shoe Box Spectroscopy

by David W. Clarke

The use of complex instruments for chemical analysis is becoming increasingly important. Unfortunately, because of school budgetary constraints, many students are not exposed to these methods until they reach the college level. When students do have access to sophisticated instruments, they often view them as black boxes, with little or no understanding of the internal workings.

The following experiment addresses both financial and technical concerns by introducing students to one example of this technology and teaching them how it works. Students are asked to construct a visible-light spectrometer using commonly available and relatively inexpensive equipment. In doing so, they are able to clearly see and understand basic spectroscopic principles and measurements.

SPECTROSCOPIC MEASUREMENT

I begin this experiment by explaining to students that when a beam of radiation (light) passes through a substance or a solution, some of the light is absorbed by the sample while the remainder is transmitted through it. The ratio of the intensity of the light entering the sample (I_o) to that exiting the sample (I_t) at a particular wavelength is defined as the transmittance (T). This is often expressed as the percent transmittance (%T), which is simply the transmittance multiplied by 100. The absorbance (A) of a sample is the negative logarithm of the transmittance:

$$\%T = (I_o/I_t) \times 100 \quad A = -log(T)$$

The absorbance of a sample at a given wavelength is proportional to the substance's absorptivity (a constant at each wavelength), the path length (the distance the light travels through the sample), and, in many instances, the concentration of the absorbing substance. In these cases the Beer-Lambert law (Skoog 1992) holds:

A	=	abc, where
a	=	absorptivity of the substance
b	=	path length
c	=	concentration of the substance

Commonly, a and b are constant for a given set of experiments so that a plot of the sample absorbance versus the concentration of the absorbing substance is a straight line. In practice, a calibration curve is prepared by plotting the absorbance of a series of standard samples as a function of their concentration. If the absorbance of an unknown sample is measured, the concentration of the absorbing component can be determined from the graph.

UV-VISIBLE SPECTROMETERS

UV-visible spectrometers are composed of four basic parts: light source, monochromator, sample holder, and detector. The most commonly used light sources produce a continuous spectrum of radiation. Because the Beer-Lambert law does not hold for multiple wavelengths, a monochromator (usually containing a prism or grating) is used in commercial spectrometers to select a single wavelength of light. The light leaving the monochromator is directed through a sample cell that contains the solution to be analyzed. A detector (normally a phototube or photomultiplier tube) is used to determine the intensity of the radiation passing through the sample. Figure 1 shows the four basic parts of a spectrometer that would be found in a typical manufactured visible-light spectrometer.

The spectrometer constructed in this experiment uses a He-Ne laser pointer as the light source. The laser pointer produces monochromatic light with a wavelength of 633 nm. This eliminates the need for a monochromator but allows only samples absorbing at this wavelength to be analyzed. Samples that absorb light at 633 nm appear green or green-blue (the complementary color of 633 nm light).

As a detector, any photocell (solar cell) and voltmeter should be acceptable. Cylindrical cuvettes or test tubes are difficult to align repeatedly in the laser beam, so it is best to use square cuvettes as sample holders. Glass or plastic cuvettes can be purchased from a catalog or fabricated from microscope slides (Gauger 1995). If standard 1 cm cuvettes are used, a hollowed-out cork can be used as a cuvette holder. The cork may not be necessary if larger cuvettes are used. A shoe box or similar size cardboard box is used to eliminate background light.

It is essential that all parts of the spectrometer be carefully aligned and then clamped or taped in place to ensure that no movement occurs between measurements and that the cuvette is reproducibly aligned. The basic parts of this spectrometer are summarized in Figure 1.

Figure 1

Comparison of a commercial spectrometer with the spectrometer constructed in the experiment

	Commercial Spectrometer	Constructed Spectrometer
Light source	Tungsten lamp	He-Ne laser
Monochromator	grating	pointer
Sample holder	round cuvette	square cuvette
Detector	phototube	photocell and voltmeter

Figure 2

Cutaway view of experimental setup

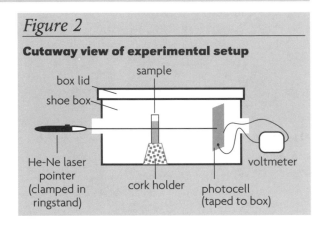

THE EXPERIMENT

A calibration curve is prepared from standard samples of green food coloring (available at grocery stores). Using this curve, the concentration of an unknown sample can be determined. Construction of the spectrometer and collection of data can be completed in less than an hour as long as the theoretical aspects of spectroscopy have been discussed in class prior to the laboratory period. Calculations and the graphing of results will add to this time.

I begin by setting up the spectrometer as shown in Figure 2. When the lid is on the shoe box, the voltmeter should read zero. If this is not the case, this background voltage must be subtracted from each reading taken. Next, I prepare a stock solution of food coloring by adding 10 drops of green food coloring to 100 ml of water. For simplicity, I treat this solution as "100% dye." This stock solution is an appropriate concentration for cuvettes with a path length of 1 cm. If 1 cm cuvettes are not used, the concentration should be adjusted using the Beer-Lambert law as a guide.

I then prepare standards with concentrations of 25, 50, and 75% dye. Students can prepare their own standards if desired. Counting drops works

Figure 3

Example data, calculated %T, and absorbance values

Absorbance	Dye concentration (%)	Reading (mv)	%T	
Blank	0	1017	100.0	0.000
Stnd. 1	100	743	73.1	0.136
Stnd. 2 (75)	832	81.8	81.8	0.087
Stnd. 3 (50)	879	86.4	86.4	0.063
Stnd. 4 (25)	943	92.7	92.7	0.032
Unknown	?	896	88.1	0.055

%T = (sample reading)/(blank reading) × 100

Absorbance = - log (%T/100)

Figure 4

Calibration curve based on the data in Figure 3

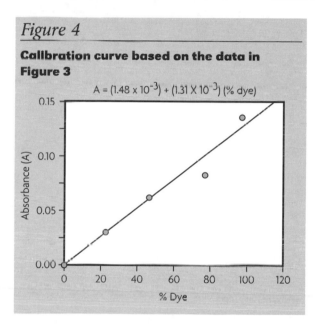

$$A = (1.48 \times 10^{-3}) + (1.31 \times 10^{-3}) \,(\% \text{ dye})$$

well (for example, a 25% dye solution can be made by mixing 25 drops of 100% dye solution with 75 drops of water). To calibrate the spectrometer, I fill a cuvette with plain water, align it in the laser beam, and read the resulting voltage. This reading is I_o—the amount of light reaching the detector when nothing is absorbing (100% of the light is transmitted).

In my classes, which are small, I prepare the 100% dye solution beforehand and let students do the rest. To begin, one student places the first standard (100%) in the sample holder and reads the voltage. This reading is I_t. Using the equations discussed earlier, students work alone to calculate the absorbance (A) for the sample. I_t is then found for the other standards (25, 50, and 75%) and the unknown, and students calculate the absorbance values for these readings. Using these values, each student then prepares a calibration curve, determines the best-fit line, and calculates the concentration of the unknown sample.

EXAMPLE DATA

A set of sample data is shown in Figure 3, and the resulting calibration curve and best-fit line are shown in Figure 4. The concentration of the unknown, as determined from the best-fit line, is 43%. With appropriate attention to detail, the accuracy of the results students get in this experiment is easily comparable to results gotten in other quantitative experiments performed in the laboratory. The most common problems encountered are too much background light, incorrect calculation of the percent transmittance, and incorrect preparation of the calibration curve.

This experiment allows students to construct a simple and inexpensive representation of an often complex and expensive piece of modern chemical instrumentation. In doing so, students are introduced to the important field of spectroscopy in an authentic fashion and, as a result, often gain a clear understanding of basic spectroscopic principles and the operation of a spectrometer.

References

Gauger, R. 1995. Using laser refractometry to determine concentration. *The Science Teacher* 62 (3):20–22.

Skoog, D.A., D.M. West, and F.J. Holler. 1992. *Fundamentals of Analytical Chemistry*. Fort Worth, TX: Saunders College Publishing.

This article first appeared in the October 1998 issue of The Science Teacher. *It was republished in the September 2006 issue, at which time the author added the following note:*

Since this article was originally published, single beam spectrometers costing less than $1,000 have become available. Unfortunately, this is still too expensive for many schools. During the same time period, the cost of red He-Ne laser pointers has also dropped to as low as $15, making the alternative described in this article even more affordable.

I have received several e-mails describing extensions to the experiment, which include analyzing copper in brass and chlorophyll in plants. The recent introduction of green laser pointers, which operate at 532 nm and are available for less than $100, opens the possibility of analyzing red to violet samples that would absorb at this wavelength.

PART

3

Teaching Strategies That Maximize the Science Budget

Chapter 12

Creative Projects Stimulate Classroom Learning

by Staci Wilson

In a perfect world, what would a good classroom strategy look like? It would have to work for any teacher at any grade level in any discipline; be backed by current research in learning theory; be elegant and simple to facilitate but differentiate for each student; be cost-effective but use a diverse selection of materials; and be active and promote inquiry. Students would be responsible for their own path to learning. They would teach and assess one another, and they would produce original, creative products. Incorporating student projects in your curriculum is one way of achieving these goals.

Classroom projects are original pieces of student work that may be in the form of art, writing, models, experiments, and various other creative outlets. Projects created and presented by students, based on units being studied, stimulate learning and give students the opportunity to follow their own interests. Brain-based learning theories uphold that classrooms that are noisy, active environments where students are engaged in individual learning paths can be conducive to students learning at high levels (Jensen 1995).

With projects, students choose their own path to learning by creating original products that are shared and displayed for others to learn from them. Students take ownership of their learning by creating products that are designed with their own individual interests, talents, and learning styles in mind. Brain-based research also suggests that when students teach what they have learned, they use their whole brain to do it, which makes long-term storage and retrieval of information more efficient.

TYPES OF PROJECTS

Projects come in a series of categories that are inclusive and flexible and offer the opportunity to be creative. Specific examples of projects include solar system models and atom models of all types, such as data collecting for a sunspot activity and posters about the rock cycle or periodic table groups. Artistic designs have included "The Lightning Song" and "The Double Binary Star Dance." Computer applications have included slide shows about native rocks and minerals and the life of Albert Einstein.

Further Reading

- "Quest Guidebooks," from the April/May 2007 issue of *The Science Teacher*
- "Periodic Table of Cereal Boxes," from the Summer 2006 issue of *The Science Teacher*

Figure 1

Project instructions for students

1. Pick a topic from the various units of study for the upcoming nine weeks, including chapters ___ of the text. These topics include _____.
2. Choose a project category from the following: models, experiments, creative writing, posters, educational tools, classic research, book or article critiques, games, computer applications, or other artistic outlets. Consider your own interests and learning styles. Pick a project that you can enjoy doing, and get approval from the teacher for your idea. All projects must be safe.
3. Sign up for your individual choice on the sign-up sheet located _____.
4. List materials needed. Determine whether the materials are available in the classroom; if not, consider whether access is available outside of school.
5. Bring all materials to class starting on _____. We will work on the projects in class for two blocks (or three 50-minute periods) only; otherwise it will be homework.
6. All projects end with a product, an oral presentation, and a three- to five-minute assessment for the audience.
7. Projects will be due according to when the individual units are close to finishing. All projects on topic _____ are due _____ and those on topic _____ are due _____.
8. The product can be almost anything. Although the challenge level of the products will be scored, the idea is to do something that will create a lasting

memory for what has been learned. Expect to spend four to six hours completing most projects, starting with research, gathering materials, product creation, and preparation of assessment. Do not forget to ask for copies or a transparency if needed.

9. Remember, the product should be a creative way to teach the audience the details of the topic. The assessment should check the audience's learning. The total time of the presentation should not be shorter than 9 minutes or exceed 15 minutes.
10. Example projects for a meteorology unit:

   • Models—atmosphere in a box, terrariums
   • Experiments—build a rain gauge and measure precipitation
   • Creative writing—poem about lightning, short story about a hurricane, children's book about seasons
   • Posters—fronts and weather systems, wind patterns
   • Educational tools—teach a mini-lesson on pressure using manipulatives
   • Classic research—write a report about Ben Franklin or lightning-strike survivors
   • Book or article critiques—write a summary about ball lightning and include pictures
   • Games—weather trivia complete with game board, instructions for play, and game pieces
   • Computer applications—create graphs on global-warming data
   • Artistic—write a song about snow, perform a rain dance for a cultural demonstration

Students enjoy making games, such as "The Great Earth Science Game" and "Chemical Trivia." Students review books like Carl Sagan's *Cosmos* and articles from *Astronomy* magazine. Creative writing comes in many forms, including a short story called "A Trip Through the Milky Way" or a fable about how the universe was created. Educational tools such as study guides and pretests are generally reserved for students considering education as a career. My personal favorite has been the songs. Students have played guitars while they sing and even performed a "doo-wop" song in Earth science that was awesome.

GETTING STARTED

To begin, prepare a list of topics you will be covering in the upcoming term and a list of suggested project

categories, and insert this information into the Project Instructions for Students sheet (Figure 1). Also insert the chapters being studied, sign-up sheet location, the date students should bring materials to class, and due dates. Hand out copies of the Project Instructions for Students to the class. Review the categories to choose from and the topic or range of topics. Emphasize that projects need to be linked to the unit being studied. Students will fill out their topic and category on a designated sign-up sheet. This can be a lined sheet of paper with name, topic, and category sections marked and positioned at a set place in the classroom. You can suggest possible project ideas, or allow students to come up with their own. It is important to limit the number of students who do similar projects; this depends entirely on how much you incorporate the projects. Projects can be incorporated one per unit as

Figure 2

Rubric for teacher to score each student's oral presentation

Name _____ Topic_____ Category_____

Product – 35 points

Creative/challenge level	10	_____
Accurate	15	_____
Attractive/high quality	5	_____
Relevant	5	_____
		_____ total

Oral Report – 45 points

Voice clear, posture good, not reading	5	_____
Appropriate length of presentation	5	_____
Depth of understanding, mastery of topic	15	_____
Strength of communication, clarity of lesson	15	_____
Can answer questions about the project	5	_____
		_____ total

Assessment – 10 points

Assesses lesson	5	_____
Clarifies concepts	5	_____
		_____ total

a culminating event or one per quarter to be presented as the various units are covered.

MATERIALS

Materials can be inexpensive, routine items that many teachers use in the classroom. Items to have in stock include poster board, sketch paper, construction paper, scissors, glue, Styrofoam, cotton, markers, glitter, toothpicks, cardboard, textbooks, magazines, and dice. Of course, the materials can be varied or limited. Students can also be responsible for bringing in their own materials. Your school library can be an invaluable resource for gaining access to magazines, books, and computers. Miscellaneous items can also come in handy, such as packing peanuts or buttons.

PROJECT PRESENTATIONS

Every project ends with an oral presentation. The presenter's goal is to tell the audience what he or she learned or clarified by doing the project. Each presenter can design a three- to five-minute assessment to see whether students in the audience learned or mastered the content from the presentation. It could be a short quiz or game; the range of possibilities is endless. If time is short, the presenter can come up with three questions for the teacher to use as a unit or topic assignment instead.

ASSESSMENT

Each member of the audience can anonymously score the presenter based on the criteria for a good learning experience, including speaking skills, depth of presentation, and creativity of the product. It can be as simple as ranking the presentations on a scale of 1 to 10, with a comment justifying the score. In addition, you can use the rubric in Figure 2 to rate each presentation yourself.

MANAGEMENT TIPS

When 30 students do 30 different activities, things can get chaotic. The noise level in the room will grow when all the students are engaged. Discuss the importance of using soft voices and limiting movement across the room. Start slowly, with one or two classes, until your organization system is in place. Make sure students understand behavior expectations and the consequences for being off task.

Have students use a sign-up sheet to track the various projects. During sign-ups, have students share aloud their ideas and progress. Although no two students should do exactly the same project, the students can feed off one anothers' ideas as their plans develop. Have a whole-group discussion at the beginning of each class so that questions are answered for everyone. This lowers the demand on the teacher for individual questions and the wait time for students. If you have a larger classroom, consider having students work in teams on projects.

If possible, show projects that have been completed in the past and tell students how they were scored. This can improve the quality of future projects. Also, limit the number of times a student can use the same category per semester. This encourages students to try new categories, which will broaden their horizons.

Make sure students know where materials are located. When most students are close to finishing, ask them to finish up the projects as homework. Allow students to take home any necessary materials needed to complete the projects at home.

During oral presentations, ask the audience to assess each presenter to keep the audience engaged and motivate the presenters. The audience can use the teacher's scoring rubric (Figure 2, p. 61) or simply rate each presentation with a number or letter grade and provide a brief explanation to justify the score.

CONCLUSION

Projects are inexpensive, active, and creative. They shift the responsibility of teaching and learning to the student. Students design their own path to learning, using their individual talents to create and share the way they learn best. The students learn at levels high enough to teach the topic, and they enjoy it. As a bonus, the products become great visual aids for future classes, if the teacher chooses to keep them.

Reference

Jensen, E. 1995. *Superteaching*. San Diego: Brain Store Inc.

This article first appeared in the October 2004 issue of Science Scope.

Chapter 13
Making Connections Fun

by Arlene Marturano

Games are a great way to help students make meaningful connections between abstract science concepts and vocabulary. The following are three games I use to help students connect, review, and reinforce what they learn in the classroom.

The game Secrets is similar to the magnetic poetry game that asks you to arrange random word magnets on your fridge to form creative sentences. In my version, the words are carefully selected to focus on a specific area of study and are written on index cards. The object of the game is for students to connect the various words in the correct order to reveal something factual (a secret) about what is being studied. For example, when we study butterflies, I provide index cards with words such as *proboscis, compound eye, nectar, wing, veins, scales,* and *barbs*. I also provide cards containing prepositions, conjunctions, and articles. It is up to students to jot down an appropriate verb on a blank index card and then arrange the cards to create a butterfly fact. For example, students might arrange the cards to say one of the following: "The butterfly has scales on the wings," "The proboscis sips nectar," or "Pairs of wings overlap."

To make a game out of it, divide the class into two teams and have a representative from each group stand at the bulletin board. Flip a coin to see who goes first, and then have that person try to make a sentence using the collection of index cards, which should be pinned to the board. The other team can then challenge the sentence if they think that it is factually incorrect. The other student can then pin up a sentence and have it judged by the opposing team. Give each team a point for a correct sentence or for correctly challenging the other team's sentence. Continue calling up pairs of students until all the cards are used up. Before removing the cards from the board, have students copy them into their notebooks to reinforce the concepts displayed.

Connections is a game requiring students to formulate relationships between pairs of concepts. During a unit on solar energy, for example, students observe the temperature and texture of apple slices baked in a foil-lined funnel cooker and an unlined funnel cooker. I write the concepts *reflect* and *absorb* on index cards, tape them to a marker board, and draw a line between them. The challenge for students is to create a sentence that explains the connection between the two concepts as it relates to the solar-cooking activity. For example, "The foil reflects heat onto the apples, which absorb it and cook." Once everyone completes their sentences, students read them aloud and we discuss if they are correct. Those students whose sentences are approved score a point and move on to the next round. At this point I add another concept to the board, such as *solar energy* or *radiation*, and those students still in the game create a new sentence that connects all three concepts. Those who are out of contention can still participate by challenging the remaining players' sentences. We continue in this fashion until only one student remains or all the concepts have been covered. For review and reinforcement, students should record all of the approved statements in their notebooks.

Pairs of Opposites is a great game to use at the end of a unit to gauge student comprehension or review before a test. To begin, have students divide up into pairs. Give each student a set of prepared index cards with vocabulary related to the unit being studied. The terms must have an opposite associated with them. (These can be created by the teacher or students, if time permits.) For example, for a meteorology unit opposite terms can include *evaporation/ condensation, warm front/cold front,* and *atmosphere/ vacuum.* For a unit on matter, you can use *melting point/freezing point, solid/liquid, organic/inorganic,* and *protons/electrons.* Students take turns revealing a term to their partners and challenging each other to come up with the appropriate opposite. Again, points can be awarded for every correct match or challenge, and the approved opposites should be recorded in students' notebooks.

This aricle first appeared in the May 2004 issue of Science Scope.

Chapter 14

Wiffle Ball Physics

by Rachael Lancor

Projectile motion, a cornerstone topic of introductory physics, is usually a student's first exposure to the problem-solving techniques used in this subject. Often, this is an inactive learning experience—students work with pencil and paper to read and solve projectile motion problems (e.g., diagrams and descriptions of balls being hit, kicked, and launched). In this activity, however, students create their own problems by applying their abstract knowledge of projectile motion to something familiar: a Wiffle ball. This activity—which can be done in one 45-minute class period—aligns with National Science Education Standards for force and motion (NRC 1996, p. 179).

PREP WORK

It is relatively easy to gather the materials needed for this activity, and Wiffle balls and bats are inexpensive to purchase. It may be interesting to have students experiment with the effect of different bats (fat versus skinny) and balls (holes versus no holes).

Students begin by working in small groups to discuss the following problem: "What information is needed to calculate the initial velocity of the ball as it is hit by the batter?" I do not provide students with a procedure to follow, but rather allow them to determine what data to collect and how to use them. Before

going outside, students in each group must show me a diagram of the problem (Figure 1) and how they propose to solve it using the projectile motion equations in the following paragraph. Often, students think to solve equations only in the horizontal direction and not the vertical—so be sure they also consider the ball's vertical motion.

Because we are not interested in the final velocity of the ball, the simplest way to solve the problem is to use the following kinematics equations for each direction.

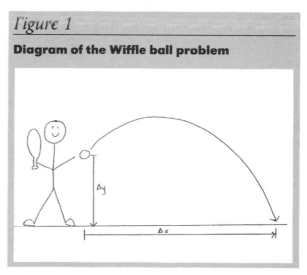

Figure 1

Diagram of the Wiffle ball problem

$$\Delta x = v_{0x}t + \frac{1}{2}a_x t^2$$

$$\Delta y = v_{0y}t + \frac{1}{2}a_y t^2$$

In these equations, Δx is the distance traveled horizontally, Δy is the distance traveled vertically, v_0 is the initial velocity, a is the acceleration, and t is time. Solving for initial velocity (v_{0x} and v_{0y}) in each direction, we get:

$$v_{0x} = \frac{\Delta x}{t}$$

$$v_{0y} = \frac{\Delta y}{t} - \frac{1}{2}a_y t$$

In these equations, a_x is assumed to be 0 and a_y is acceleration due to gravity (or -9.8 m/s²). (Note: Of course, students may choose to use the other kinematics equations to solve the problem [e.g., $v = v_0 + at$ and $v^2 = v_0^2 + 2a \Delta x$], but they will end up with the same answer.) Students need to measure horizontal distance traveled (Δx), vertical distance traveled (Δy; a student's shoulder height is a good approximation), and time spent in the air (t). In most cases, Δx will be positive and Δy will be negative. (Note: Students often miss that the change in height is negative.) Their measurements can be used to calculate the initial velocity of the ball in each direction.

After finding the velocity in the horizontal and vertical directions, students use vector analysis to find the total initial velocity (Figure 2). They can determine both the velocity of the ball and the angle at which it was hit. Students find the total velocity of the ball using the Pythagorean theorem and the angle using the trigonometric functions (Figure 2).

PLAYING BALL

When students have outlined the problem correctly and decided what data to collect, they go outdoors—where there is ample space for them to spread out—to collect data. I review safety guidelines for throwing and hitting balls and advise students not to fool around and to use caution when others are nearby.

In groups of four, each student is assigned a role: hitter, pitcher, timer, or measurer. The timer times how long the ball is in the air after it leaves the bat. The batter should not move after hitting the ball so that an accurate starting position can be obtained for the distance measurement. The measurer takes note of where the ball first lands (not where the ball rolls to) and measures the horizontal distance from the batter to

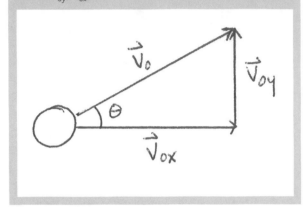

Figure 2

Vector components of the hit ball
Students calculate the total velocity of the batted ball (v_0) using the Pythagorean theorem ($v_0^2 = v_{0x}^2 + v_{0y}^2$), and the angle ($\theta$) using trigonometric functions (e.g., $\tan \theta = v_{0y}/v_{0x}$).

this point; he or she also measures the vertical distance, approximately from the batter's shoulder to the ground. Students take turns until everyone has had a chance to assume each role. For best results, students should play on level ground. Otherwise, they must take height differences (between the starting and landing point ground level) into account when calculating Δy (Figure 3).

SOLVING FOR INITIAL VELOCITY

After students have collected their data, they solve for the initial velocity of the ball. Clearly, this activity is a simplification of a very complicated problem. However, even though air friction and rotational motion are significant in the movement of the Wiffle ball, the effects of friction and spin can be neglected without compromising the integrity of the investigation as a learning experience. Students' calculations of velocity may not be accurate, but they are useful for starting a discussion about projectile motion, drag forces, how drag would affect the velocity, and how drag force changes with different balls.

In addition to the calculations, I ask students to qualitatively answer the following questions based on the investigation:

1. Is the velocity calculation you made accurate? What else would you measure to get a better value?
2. How would the problem change if someone caught the ball, or if it landed in the stands?
3. How does the angle at which you hit the ball affect the time it spends in the air and the distance traveled?

4. How does the velocity at which you hit the ball affect the time it spends in the air and the distance traveled?
5. You have not measured the following variables, but think about their relationship to the velocity of the ball hit. How do you think the ball's velocity is affected by

- the velocity of the pitched ball?
- the speed of the bat?
- a strong wind blowing toward you?
- a strong wind blowing away from you?
- using a tennis ball instead of a Wiffle ball?

Extensions allow students to delve deeper into the subject of projectile motion. For introductory students, questions 4 and 5 can be answered more qualitatively through detailed experiments and the results can be graphed for further analysis. Also, video analysis of the ball can illustrate the effects of drag and rotational motion. For more advanced students, the drag on the Wiffle ball can be included for a more accurate calculation of its velocity. The drag coefficient varies between 0.4 and 0.6, depending on the way the ball is thrown (Rossman and Rau 2007). In addition, students can account for rotational inertia to obtain a more accurate measurement of their balls' speed. The rotational inertia for a hollow ball of mass (M) and radius (R)

$$(I = \frac{2}{3} MR^2)$$

is easiest to take into account if the problem is solved using conservation of energy.

ACTIVE LEARNING

In physics, many experiments involve verifying known quantities, such as the acceleration due to gravity. These experiments can be frustrating to students when they do not get the "right answer." In this experiment, however, there is not one right answer, and students can be successful regardless of how they hit the ball. Through this simple activity, students practice solving projectile motion problems and have fun in the process. Students' active role in the creation and solution of the problem makes this a valuable learning experience.

References

National Research Council (NRC). 1996. *National science education standards.* Washington, DC: National Academies Press.
Rossman, J., and A. Rau. 2007. An experimental study of Wiffle ball aerodynamics. *American Journal of Physics* 75 (21): 1099–1105.

This article first appeared in the September 2009 issue of The Science Teacher.

Figure 3

The vertical height traveled changes when the ground is not level.

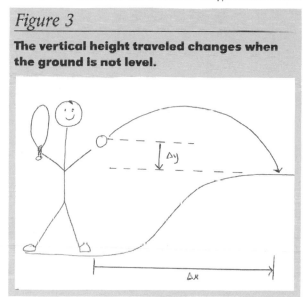

Chapter 15

Survivor Science

Out Observe. Out Measure. Out Analyze.

by Kathy Costello

C an you imagine yourself in the outback or on a tropical island, using your scientific smarts to outwit all the others? Are there times when you would just like to yell at the screen, "If you would just remember what you learned in eighth-grade science, you would have had a fire started by now!" Now there's an idea! Why not challenge students to use what we've taught them in a setting that tests their skills of science and survival? I have developed such a plan, called "Survivor Science."

Survivor Science is a weeklong activity that grabs the attention of even the most learning-resistant middle level student. Originally planned as an authentic assessment tool, it could also be used to introduce a multitude of units and is easily adapted to any scientific discipline that you teach. One "day" on the "island" fits into a 45-minute class period.

Further Reading

- "Take the Eco-Challenge," from the Summer 2005 issue of *Science and Children*
- "Ecosystem Jenga," from the September 2009 issue of *Science Scope*

WRITING THE SCRIPT

Preparations start a week in advance. First, find an area that suits your needs. It's more fun if you can leave the classroom for the activities, even if it's only to a section of the grounds that have been roped off. Our school is located on the edge of a park, so we use the picnic pavilion for our "island." If you can't get outside, try using a multipurpose room, corner of the gym, stage, or empty classroom. Just changing the decorations in your classroom to give it a jungle atmosphere helps the students feel this is special. Two such important decorations are the immunity idol and the torch. The tribe with the most points each day carries the idol, so make it something sturdy and scientific. Ours is a large paperweight that has thick syrup oozing from one side to the other.

The right props are also needed for the dramatic moment when a torch is put out. You can purchase or borrow backyard bamboo torches, available at garden stores for about $2 a piece. If you're going to be inside, or if you're not sure how your students will act around a lit torch, skip the liquid fuel and replace the wicks with red and orange yarn to resemble flames.

Next, choose the skills that you wish to test and the activities for testing them. The challenges are

CAUTION

adaptations of games, so keep the format simple and fun (see Figure 1 for suggestions). It is helpful to have a script to read that includes the day's directions, reminders about behavior, and other announcements. If you're headed outside, the activities should be no more than 30 minutes long to allow time for the walk to the site, explanations of the rules, and a tribal council vote afterward. You'll want to have a few activities that are easily adapted for indoor use in case of inclement weather.

Make sure the activities are easily graded because you will need to tally the points quickly after the task has been completed. One way to achieve this is to give each tribe an answer sheet after the challenge is complete so they can circle the correct responses. Another way is to mark a checklist as skills in the challenge have been completed.

If you're counting the challenge as a grade, everyone in the tribe gets the same grade—an excellent incentive for good teamwork. Because this activity is used as an assessment tool, the concepts and skills tested are those the students have previously learned. If each challenge is worth 20 points, students take the equivalent of a 100-point test by the end of a week. The tribe (that has not already been voted off the island) with the most points for the day's challenge has immunity at tribal council.

Supplies vary depending on the challenge activities chosen. Most challenges are based on familiar hands-on science activities that can be done with the usual classroom supplies, so the cost is minimal. The biggest expense is the prizes, which can be adjusted to fit your budget. Also, your school's PTA or a community organization may be willing to help fund the project for you.

The daily clue, while not necessary to the learning experience, adds to the students' fun. Just as participants on the television show get their "jungle mail" with hints about the next challenge, student survivors hear a rhyming clue each morning to get them thinking early in the day. Prepare one for each activity if you wish.

TRIBAL TEENAGERS

The week before the game begins, divide the castaways into teams of three to five students. The students are then given one class period to prepare for their island adventure. Each team uses the internet and other resources to research and choose a tribal name. It may have some significance to the topic being studied, or it may be an ancient name that fits the tribe's personality. One tribe chose "Rock Lords" for a geology survivor week. Another

named themselves "Papinashwash," which means "the laughing people."

Most important, each tribe hands in a sealed envelope that contains a list of 10 items from the science lab that they want to take to the island to help them survive the challenges of the days ahead. This is the only equipment they are allowed to take with them. What they choose could give their tribe an advantage over the others. They have to write their list in the clear and precise language of science and include basics such as pencils and paper. Anything readily available in the lab that is not breakable or expensive and can fit in a sack is allowed (i.e., plastic beakers, tape, metersticks, hand lenses, etc.). If a tribe is not careful about writing the exact name or quantity of the equipment, the members may find that they get what is written, not necessarily what they wanted. For example, a tribe that wrote "litmus paper" got only one strip in their sack. The tribe that carelessly wrote "cylinder" was given a toilet paper tube—not the graduated cylinder they were going to use to measure liquids. They are warned that the teacher has the final say and, if they make an unreasonable request (e.g., "computer" or "10 rolls of duct tape"), they lose that item and their list of survival supplies shrinks.

The day before the challenges begin, the teacher assembles the equipment orders from available items in the lab and labels the bags with each tribe's name. Sacks are kept in the classroom when they're not in use. Checking them at the end of each day is a good way to make sure nothing has been lost, broken, or added during each day's challenge.

TO THE ISLAND!

Surviving on an island shore
Means back to basics—nothing more.
Identify without a doubt
A compound you can't live without.
If you provide for your thirsty crew:
Your pick of Root Beer, Coke, or Dew.

Each morning during homeroom time, "jungle mail" is delivered to the participating students. They know the challenges can cover anything that we've discussed over the past month (or any length of time or unit you choose), but if they can figure out the clue they have an advantage over the other tribes. Last-minute reviews and lunchtime cram sessions are encouraged. When it's time for science class, the tribes gather their survivor sacks and torches and head for the "island." The walk to the island can be perilous. That's the time when alliances are made and broken on the

Figure 1

Sample challenges

Botany

1. Using the words that describe the characteristics of plants, the tribes describe native plants and write a dichotomous key to be used for the remainder of their stay on the island.
2. On the island, monocots are edible and dicots are poisonous. Given samples of various roots, leaves, stems, seeds, and flowers, tribes must choose 10 plants that are edible.
3. Using clues and keys, students identify plants that could be used for making rope, repelling insects, building shelter, and other tasks essential to living in the wild.
4. When one of the tribe is "injured," the rest of the group uses their knowledge of plant parts to find the roots that stop bleeding, the tuber that counteracts the poison, and the rhizoid that cures the life-threatening allergy.
5. A tribe member is kidnapped and the only clue left is part of a plant. Using their dichotomous key and a map of the island, the rest of the tribe follows a treasure hunt of clues to rescue their friend.

Ecology

1. Given a sample of muddy water, the tribe has to find a way to get it as clean as possible with the available supplies.
2. Tribes must diagram a food pyramid of the island's plant and animal species to determine how many plants and animals they can safely consume each day without causing a crash in the island's sensitive populations.
3. When told that a dangerous castaway-eating beast populates the island, the tribes must devise protective strategies for themselves similar to those found in nature.
4. Students are caught in the center of a giant web that restricts their survival efforts. For example, a web thread labeled "Build a shelter for your group" is tied to "Plants you removed leave area of bare soil," "Increased erosion to stream," and "Silt buildup covers clam food source." Tribes have to find a way out of the web by cutting the fewest number of threads.
5. Tribes race to find envelopes that represent animal food sources. They have to be careful because the names of the animals are not familiar. Inside the envelopes are cards that tell if the animal is an herbivore, predator, parasite, etc.

Geology

1. Each tribe is given scraps of paper in unusual shapes. On one side is a map of the geologic features of the island that will be crucial to their survival. On the other side is a diagram of the rock cycle. Students use their knowledge of the cycle to be the first to complete the map.
2. The native people of the island are angered by the tribe's presence. They kidnap one member of each tribe. With only a rock sample for a clue, the tribes use their maps to find their missing tribe members.
3. To find the raw materials they need for the rest of the week, tribes use scratch plates, Moh's hardness scale, and other techniques to identify various useful rocks found on the island.
4. The groups must use their knowledge of the features of karst topography to find their way through an "a-mazing" cave system to their food supply.
5. A mining company has come to the island to mine a deposit of a rare mineral. Their operations may disrupt the delicate balance of life on the island and disturb the native people. Tribes use their maps to make their recommendations to the mining company. The tribe that has the most reasons with the most facts to support those reasons wins immunity.

Chemistry

1. Students use paper circles labeled "proton," "neutron," and "electron" to construct models of the given elements. The tribe that correctly completes the most models in 15 minutes is granted immunity.
2. Tribes identify elements in solution by using a flame test. They arrange the elements in the correct atomic number order to break a code that gives the password to gain immunity.
3. Survivors race to raise the temperature of a beaker of water. The tribe that has the greatest rise in temperature wins.
4. Tribes tackle a "treasure hunt" where the clues are the numbers of the periodic table. They must translate the numbers into the symbols that spell out the clue.
5. Given a variety of vials filled with white powders and clear liquids, the tribe must pick only four vials to make two chemical reactions.

Physics

1. Tribes are informed that on this island, the laws of gravity are suspended for 15 minutes each day at an unpredictable time. They have to list five things they expect to happen at that time and how they plan to use or combat those effects to help them complete a given task.
2. A volcano erupts, sending a flow of lava toward the encampment. The rickety raft given to each tribe holds only one person at a time. Teams must use Newton's $f = ma$ calculation to find out how much force must be used to push each person's mass across the gap to safety.
3. A giant eagle that inhabits the island is known to eat humans. It gives a loud caw when it sees its prey, then dives at a given speed from a given height. Tribes must calculate the speed they must run to reach the shelter from five different points on the island to survive the eagle's attacks.
4. Each tribe is given a collection of odds and ends. Team members must use their knowledge of simple machines to build a device that helps the group survive.
5. The natives send a collection of the compound machines they have devised to perform various tasks on the island. Tribes must analyze the machines, listing the simple machines that are used in each one. They must also describe when the machine reaches its maximum potential energy and its maximum kinetic energy.

basis of who is being helpful and who isn't. Alliances and grudges are allowed; however, the students are reminded that all school rules are strictly enforced. Tribes may borrow and share equipment with other tribes if they think that can improve their chances of staying on the island.

A JUNGLE OF CHALLENGES

Upon arriving at the island each day, students are given a challenge to overcome, the outcome of which determines their fate. For example:

"You're all really thirsty. Each tribe has five bottles of clear liquids. Only one of them is water. Your challenge is to prove which one is safe to drink without endangering any of the members of your tribe. You must have two different ways to prove that the liquid you choose is water. You must also have two ways to prove the other liquids are not water. To assist you in that challenge, I have some tools for you in numbered bags. You may only have two items. Your tribe will write down the numbers of two of the bags, and I will give you one of each of the items in those bags. I will not hand out any of the items until I have the written list from each tribe. You may pour the liquids into any containers you have in your survival sack. Use the safe lab techniques you've learned when handling these liquids: waft to smell them, do NOT touch them or drink them. Goggles on? Tribes ready? Go!"

In this chemistry challenge, four bottles contain diluted (20%) solutions of vinegar, bleach, sodium hydroxide, and sulfuric acid. The final bottle contains water. The mystery bags contain pH paper, red litmus paper, blue litmus paper, purple cabbage juice, and baking soda. The students receive only two of them to help determine the acidity of the liquids. Tribes that requested litmus paper on their supply list have the advantage for this task.

Each day the winning tribe takes possession of the coveted immunity idol and is safe from the vote at tribal council. Another incentive, in addition to immunity, is that each day's task is worth points earned toward a final grade.

YOU MUST LEAVE THE ISLAND IMMEDIATELY

At the end of each class period's challenge, the tribal council convenes to vote a team off the island. Important here is the fact that *tribes* are voted off, not individuals. This prevents hurt feelings and keeps the number of days devoted to the project to a minimum.

The torches are lit for the tribal council. There's last-minute bargaining and alliance forging as the tribes huddle to discuss their votes. Each tribe is allowed only one vote, so sometimes there's vigorous debate before all members of a tribe agree. Tribes write their choices on jungle parchment (brown construction paper) and place their vote in the ballot box. Each class period ends with the teacher counting the votes until the fateful words "The tribes have spoken" are uttered, and another torch is extinguished.

All the tribes participate in the voting, no matter if they have already been voted off the island or not. Tribes that are voted off the island still perform the remaining challenges and can win daily prizes as they add points to their grade, but they cannot be the final survivors. If a tribe wins a challenge but has already been voted off, the first eligible tribe that completes the task successfully wins immunity. Tribes already off the island find it amusing to annoy and confound the remaining tribes, adding new depth to the definition of the word *survival*. As long as the usual school rules for respectful behavior are followed, anything goes.

THE TRIBES HAVE SPOKEN

Each day another challenge is completed. Each day another torch is put out. Each day a different tribe hears "You must leave the island immediately." Each day the number of tribes eligible for the pizza party dwindles. But each day interest in science burns brighter. Students have been known to organize study sessions and brag about everything they have already learned for the next day's challenge. That's right, eighth graders ... studying ... in May. Unbelievable. Not only do students discover that science applies to everyday challenges, they also discover the ability in themselves to meet those challenges. They come to appreciate science not as a problem to be endured, but as a way to find the solutions to life.

This article first appeared in the May 2004 issue of Science Scope.

Chapter 16

History of Science Poster Challenge

by Elizabeth James

The history and nature of science—National Science Education Content Standard G (NRC 1996, pp. 200–204)—is a theme commonly neglected in the science classroom. Students often recognize only a few of the great names in science and even then their perception of the scientists may be vague. The image of a physicist as a myopic older white male is nearly universal. Learners fail to see scientists as multidimensional human beings or to understand their work in historical perspective. Textbooks rarely supply more information than a picture, some dates, and a thumbnail sketch of a few well-known scientists' work. The following activity gives students an opportunity to get up close and personal with a scientist and to share their discoveries in a creative and interesting format.

To learn more about the history of science, my secondary level physics students began their second semester by choosing a physicist to nominate to the "Physicist Hall of Fame." The project ultimately involved two student products: a persuasive paper describing the physicist's work and why the physicist should be included in the Hall of Fame, and a lab poster to represent the physicist in our Hall of Fame.

RESEARCH

No two students were permitted to investigate the same physicist. I gave students no hints as to how to pick a physicist and I allowed them to define "physicist" loosely, merely pointing out that they would have to justify the nomination. Students researched their physicists and created their products entirely outside of class time. Students were encouraged to use the internet to gather information about their scientists; they had internet access through the media center and my classroom computer. Students were required to have bibliographies of at least three sources, including

Figure 1

Examples of student posters

at least one non-internet source. I have been working toward building a physics library for my classroom, which also served as a somewhat limited resource.

PERSUASIVE PAPERS AND TAB POSTERS

The paper was a persuasive writing assignment written according to the format studied this year as part of our school improvement accreditation goals (North Central Accreditation). In addition to describing the physicist's work, each paper needed to justify the scientist's inclusion in the Physicist Hall of Fame. The papers contained important dates such as birth, death, and years of significant achievements (e.g., dates of Nobel prizes and publication of important works). In addition to biographical data, a brief description of each physicist's contributions to science was required. A specific page length was not defined, but students were instructed that the length should be appropriate to the amount of information they were presenting.

The next part of the assignment was to create a tab poster that is made of medium-weight poster board. The focal point of the poster had to represent some characteristics of the physicists or their research. (Hint: Students should not make the focal point too obvious!) Students cut 11 three-sided openings in the poster board to form flaps and numbered 10 of the flaps 1 through 10 (Figures 1, p. 75, and 2). Under each of the flaps students pasted a paper on which they had typed or neatly written a fact about their scientists, with the most obscure fact being flap 1 and the most obvious fact being flap 10. The idea was to have viewers begin with flap 1, read the facts about the scientist in succession, and try to guess who it was. The last flap, which was unnumbered, hid the name of the scientist. The posters were arranged and decorated to be interesting and visually appealing.

The paper and poster were evaluated separately. The combined scores of the two products were equivalent to a test grade. The rubric I used to evaluate the paper and poster is given in Figure 3. Posters were displayed in the hallway as they were turned in. The poster presentation coincided with parent-teacher conferences; the posters also attracted

Figure 2

A student tab poster representing J. Robert Oppenheimer
Behind each numbered flap is a clue to the physicist's identity. The poster is designed to look like an atom, with the clues representing electrons. The quote "Science is not everything, but science is very beautiful" is attributed to Oppenheimer.

the attention of other students and staff. As a result, a great deal of information about physicists was disseminated to people beyond our classroom.

PROBLEMS ENCOUNTERED

The main difficulty with this project was that students had trouble understanding the mechanics of the poster. I finally created a poster as an example; I also saved several student posters as examples for next year's project. Some students did not like the suggestion that they should cut tabs from their posters and instead used construction paper to create flaps. This approach worked well except that the flaps did not hold up as well to repeated lifting. Another problem was wall space. Because each student created a poster, some posters had to be mounted high on the walls and the flaps were not accessible for the higher posters. In some areas, the amount of flammable material allowed on walls is limited by fire regulations, so be sure to check with your local authorities.

GETTING INVESTED

Students appreciated the opportunity to be creative and enjoyed trying to guess the scientists in the poster challenge. I found that students became quite invested in their physicists' accomplishments because they had to persuade others of the value of their chosen scientists' work. Some minority students were able to discover scientists who shared their heritage. Other students uncovered bizarre

Figure 3

Assessment rubric

Paper:	Points
Typed or neatly handwritten	5
Includes pertinent biographical information	10
Correct description of physicist's work	20
Persuasive writing format	10
Bibliography	5
Total possible	**50**

Poster:	Points
Visually appealing	10
Ten appropriate facts	10
Facts arranged in logical order	10
Representative symbol	10
Neat and legible	5
Turned in on time	5
Total possible	**50**

facts about their physicist; it was interesting to see what facts were chosen and in what order they were arranged.

This assignment encouraged good problem solving as students discovered the best resources to find information about scientists and defined just what constitutes a physicist. I noticed a lot of cooperation among students who shared web resources and made suggestions to peers on how to design posters. The project incorporated a variety of intelligences and learning styles and provided an opportunity for physics students to learn about important figures in the history of science.

Reference

National Research Council (NRC). 1996. *National science education standards*. Washington, DC: National Academies Press.

This article first appeared in the February 2005 issue of The Science Teacher.

Chapter 17

Cartooning Your Way to Student Motivation

by Derek Sallis, Audrey C. Rule, and Ethan Jennings

Unmotivated, underachieving students pose a huge challenge for teachers. One way to motivate and stimulate student interest in a topic is to use humor. Humor can help students make new connections in learning and improves retention of information (Garner 2006). In this article, we describe how we integrated art and literature with science to encourage curiosity through the exploration of rocks, crystals, and fossils; to fuel interest with science trade books; and to translate newly acquired science information into funny cartoons.

Analyzing, improving, and creating cartoons related to science content has been shown to increase both science achievement and student motivation in a study of sixth graders learning about rocks and minerals (Rule and Auge 2005). Interestingly, a study on the efficacy of cigarette warning labels (Duffy 1999) showed that the addition of a cartoon figure to the warning increased the believability of health consequences for adolescents. In addition, creativity gives Americans a competitive edge in the global economy against other countries with equally technically skilled workers (Zhao 2008). Yager (2000, p. 337), in his vision of reformed and effective science education for the year 2025, lamented, "Much research and development has been done on developing students' abilities in this creative domain, but little of this has been purposely incorporated into science programs."

The cartoon-making activities described here (see Activity Instruction Sheet, p. 83) engage students while they learn Earth science concepts and develop their abilities to visualize and combine ideas in new ways. Our diverse classroom population of African American, Latino, and white middle school students enrolled in a class for reading enrichment and improvement enjoyed the activity, remaining almost glued to the tasks for the entire class period. (See the cartoons they created, Figures 1 and 2, pp. 80 and 81.)

ENGAGING STUDENTS THROUGH SIGHT AND TOUCH

We began by providing hands-on materials to focus student attention and to engage tactile learners. We provided rock samples with interesting textures, glittering

Further Reading

- "The Art of Physics: Using Cartooning to Illustrate Newton's Laws of Motion," from the December 2008 issue of *The Science Teacher* crystals, and "cool" fossils such as a reproduction of a dinosaur footprint and some intricately detailed horn corals. We also provided vesicle-filled lava rock samples and a stalactite from the blast zone of a remodeled commercial cave entrance (remind students to never touch or remove stalactites from natural caves). Eye-catching mineral samples and fossils are often sold in museum gift shops, science stores, and rock shops. Alternatively, you could invite a guest speaker to visit and show specimens from a collection.

Allow students, who are seated in small groups for all of the activities described in this article, a few minutes to examine the materials and talk to peers about what they notice or know about them. Ask students to sketch two specimens that they find interesting and record their observations. Call on volunteers to share observations and infer the origin of the specimens, providing additional information as needed so that all students have a basic understanding of the main features of the items.

Our students were fascinated with the materials. They recognized the dinosaur footprint but were less able to identify the other fossils. This initial formative assessment provided us with information about students' background knowledge so that we could better support their learning. Because our work was conducted as guests in a remedial *literacy* (rather than science) class, we did not have the opportunity to conduct earlier lessons to build a stronger foundation for learning about these Earth science topics; however, many of our students made connections to previous science lessons. You may want to extend this lesson over several days with your students.

READING EXCITING TEXTS

After student interest was piqued through examination of specimens, we provided Earth science content information to them through richly illustrated texts written at a range of grade levels. We used nonfiction picture books written for elementary and middle school audiences, although more technical texts, field guides, or coffee-table books can be used if they have colorful, exciting pictures. Because this lesson took place in a class for struggling and easily frustrated readers, it was important to provide highly visual books with short text passages so that comprehension was supported with images.

We brought a large selection of books so that students would have ample choices from which to find a book that ignited their curiosity and presented textual information at an independent reading level (hence the large number of elementary books). We used books that focused on minerals and crystals, volcanoes, earthquakes, glaciers, caves, and dinosaurs or

Figure 1

Polar pinball

Global climate change brings dangerous changes to Earth. The polar ice is already melting.

other fossils. In this way, students could choose books that focused on their particular Earth science interests. You might supplement what is available in your school library with books that you check out from your local public library for this in-class activity. Be sure to provide enough books so that students have a lot of choice and can switch to other books when they have finished reading or if they realize that the book is too difficult or not of interest. Ideally, have twice as many books as students.

We asked students to find a book of interest and to read silently for 20 minutes. To help them quickly choose appealing books, we sorted the books by topic and connected these with many of the specimens students had just explored. Our students were eager to browse the books because of their interesting illustrations, some of which matched the samples we had supplied. They began by paging through and reading excerpts; soon they were fully engaged in reading. They read silently and individually for 20 minutes, pausing occasionally to show classmates interesting facts or images in the books. After 20 minutes, we asked students to talk to group members about what they had learned. Then students recorded a few facts, using complete sentences, in their notebooks.

ANALYZING EARTH SCIENCE CARTOONS

After they looked at the books, we told students that soon they would make cartoons that incorporated content related to minerals and crystals, volcanoes, earthquakes, glaciers, caves, or fossils, using humor to

Figure 2

Glacial meltdown

I see a lot of melting in your future.

Glenda Glacier was not at all pleased with the forecast for more global climate change.

convey their newly acquired Earth science content from the reading. To prepare for the cartoon making and to inspire students, we showed them colorful, funny cartoon examples related to these same Earth science topics made by preservice teachers (Rule, Sallis, and Donaldson 2008), available free online (see References for a link to the article and cartoons). Each of these cartoons is accompanied by an explanation of the pertinent science content. We printed a color set of the cartoons with their explanations from the article appendix and circulated them among groups of students.

We gave students time to read the cartoons and enjoy the humor. Then we asked each group to choose two cartoons and explain to the rest of the class the science content and sources of humor. Humor often depends on wordplay such as homophones (e.g., *dear* and *deer*) or words with multiple meanings (e.g., *play*: to toy with an object, a dramatic skit, or a sports move), exaggerated emotions, impossible situations, or parody. Some classic books that illustrate common puns are the series written and illustrated by Fred Gwynne, who played Herman Munster in the popular TV series *The Munsters* (see Resources for more information). If time permits, you may want to use these and other books suggested by your language arts colleagues or school librarian to build a foundation for recognizing and creating humorous wordplay.

MAKING ORIGINAL CARTOONS

The goal for this activity is to help students take Earth science concepts that they have learned through

reading nonfiction trade books and to re-communicate them to others through the medium of humorous or clever cartoons. The NSES Science Content Standards state that more emphasis should be placed on "communicating science explanations" (NRC 1996, p. 113). This cartoon-making activity allows students to integrate literacy, science, and art for the purpose of communicating science learning. As in the other activities, students should be seated in small groups of three to five. Students may work individually on a cartoon or with one or more members of the group. Each student or team of students might begin a cartoon and continue working on it with input from other group members.

To ensure that a solid content foundation is being established, ask students to begin by writing a statement of the science information that will be conveyed by the cartoon they make. This might be one of the fact statements that they wrote after reading a trade book. Sometimes, as in the "polar pinball" cartoon example (Figure 1), this statement becomes the caption of the cartoon. Other times, the science ideas are inferred from the cartoon visuals and caption. We exposed our students to a wide range of Earth science topics through the specimens, trade books, and example cartoons because we wanted them to choose topics of high interest for reading and designing cartoons. You may want to reduce the number of topics to fit more closely with what your students are studying. The example cartoon resource discussed here provides several samples for each of the six topic areas; therefore, students will have models even if your focus is narrower.

As stated in the *National Science Education Standards'* Science Teaching Standards, "Student understanding is actively constructed through individual and social processes" (NRC 1996, p. 29). A student clarifies thoughts while explaining them to others and receives helpful feedback and fresh ideas from classmates. Students may want to brainstorm, in groups or as a whole class, science words related to what they have just read that have homophones or multiple meanings to help in creating humor. For example, some possible terms for wordplay are *order, quartz, crystal, model* (crystals); *Old Faithful, explode, dormant, sleeping, erupt* (volcanoes); *Richter scale, fault, shocking, shaker, crack-up, love waves* (earthquakes); *calving, freezing on, terminal moraine* (glaciers); *cast, mold, bone to pick* (fossils); and *deposit, bank, cave, batty* (caves). Identifying the puns used in the example cartoons from "Humorous Cartoons Made by Preservice Teachers for Teaching Science Concepts to Elementary Students: Process and Product" (Rule, Sallis, and Donaldson 2008) can also be beneficial. We didn't have any problems with inappropriate jokes or drawings, but you may want to remind students of the limits of acceptable humor: No cartoons that insult classmates, teachers, or groups; no foul language; no violence or sexual content.

Provide color printouts of background scenarios on which students can add hand-drawn characters, talking bubbles, details, and captions to make their cartoons, like those shown in Figure 3. We used clip art in PowerPoint to make familiar or fantasy scenes of human experience and then printed them for students: a hospital operating room, a fortune-teller, a birthday party room, a pinball arcade, a snack shop, a UFO with a beam extending to the ground, the stacks in a library, a talk-show host on the stage, an open scrapbook page, the dance floor in front of a rock band, and an open tent at a campground. To save paper, you might provide each group of students with a set of two to four backgrounds, rather than printing them all for individual students. We found that providing prompts for each setting helped students generate ideas. For example, with the scrapbook setting, we asked, "What Earth science event would your Earth feature want to remember with a scrapbook page?" Students then decorated the scrapbook page, perhaps including a definition of a science term for their personified Earth feature. For a talk-show setting, we asked, "What funny things happened or were discussed when your Earth feature appeared on a TV talk show?" Also allow students to generate their own original settings for cartoons. Supply colored pencils to make the task more interesting and the results more colorful; having erasable colored pencils so that students can easily refine their work is even better.

Students should be allowed access to the texts throughout their cartoon work to find additional information, check facts, clarify ideas, or find details. As students work, misunderstandings they have about their newly acquired science knowledge may appear in their cartoon drawings or captions. An article in *Science Scope* (Song et al. 2008) detailed several ways to use cartoons in assessing student science understandings. As recommended by the authors of that article, classmates might explain their alternate understandings of "controversial" cartoon situations (cartoons showing science facts or processes about which there is disagreement among students as to correctness) and offer evidence from texts to support their reasoning.

As you interact with students, tell them specifically what they are doing effectively and make suggestions for additional components they may want to add to make the concepts clearer. The work can be started on one day and completed at a later class period or for

Figure 3

Background examples

What type of books would your Earth feature check out of the library?
What happens when your Earth feature goes to the library?

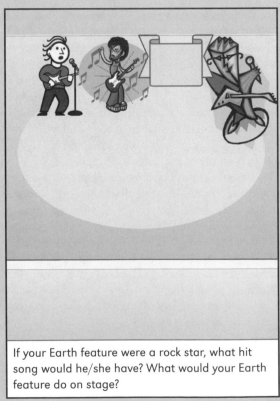

If your Earth feature were a rock star, what hit song would he/she have? What would your Earth feature do on stage?

Activity Instruction Sheet

Overview: In this art-literacy-science integrated activity, students explore Earth science objects, read informational books to learn more, examine humorous science cartoons others have made, and then create funny cartoons of their own that communicate science facts.

1. Engaging students through sight and touch **Materials:** Several rock, mineral, and fossil specimens with interesting textures, lusters, or features **Objective:** Students focus their attention on Earth science while making observations of specimens and discussing their knowledge or interests with peers. **Time:** 10–15 minutes Provide specimens of interesting rocks, minerals, and fossils to students seated in small groups. Students examine items and suggest to classmates what they are and how they formed. After activating this prior knowledge, volunteers tell observations and inferences to the whole group. The teacher or guest speaker fills in additional information about the origin of each specimen and answers questions.	**2. Reading exciting texts** **Materials:** A large variety of richly illustrated nonfiction books at elementary and middle school reading levels that focus on Earth science topics **Objective:** Students read silently and independently for 20 minutes and then record several sentences of Earth science facts that they learned from reading. **Time:** 25 minutes Students choose books of interest that focus on various Earth science topics, including minerals and crystals, volcanoes, earthquakes, glaciers, caves, and dinosaurs or other fossils. They read silently for 20 minutes. Then they tell students in their groups two or three interesting facts that they learned and record these ideas in their notes.
3. Analyzing Earth science cartoons **Materials:** Color printouts of the cartoons and explanations from the appendix of the Rule, Sallis, and Donaldson article (2008) **Objective:** Students examine cartoons stating the science content and the source of humor. **Time:** 15 minutes Pass out color copies of the cartoons with their accompanying science content explanations. After students have had a chance to look at the cartoons and read the science explanations, assign two cartoons for each group to analyze for science content and sources of humor. Groups report this information to the class. Humor often depends on puns (homophones, words with multiple meanings), parody, exaggerated expressions, and ridiculous situations.	**4. Making original cartoons** **Materials:** Clip-art background scenes for cartoons, erasable colored pencils **Objective:** Students write a science fact to be communicated by a cartoon. They choose a cartoon setting and add details to complete a humorous cartoon. **Time:** 15–30 minutes Ask students to record the fact(s) that they would like to use when illustrating their cartoons. Provide cartoon setting ideas with clip-art scenes and accompanying questions. Students should tell group members their ideas and obtain additional suggestions of puns or humorous situations from them. Remind students of the limits of acceptable humor: No cartoons that insult classmates, teachers, or groups; no foul language; no violence or sexual content. Then students should choose a setting and add characters, details, call-outs, a caption, and a title.

homework, as students often need incubation time for generating creative ideas.

SHARING AND ASSESSMENT

It's nice to share completed cartoons, perhaps by posting them on a bulletin board, so that students can demonstrate their accomplishments. Because of limited access to computers, our students turned in hand-drawn work and we translated their sketches to clip art or scanned and traced their images to make the final cartoons shown here. However, there are electronic ways for students to produce cartoons that can be effective if they have access to software: Students might add to given clip-art backgrounds in PowerPoint by using drawing tools or additional clip art, or use other drawing applications, such as Comic Life, to create original cartoons.

A rubric for scoring student work might include the following criteria: (1) statement of science content displayed by the cartoon; (2) explanation of why the cartoon is funny or clever, perhaps including a play on words; (3) sufficient details drawn (talking bubbles, characters, captions, color, elaborations) to make the cartoon understandable; and (4) visual appeal.

CONCLUSION

This technique was successful in motivating underachieving students to read science books and practice communicating the information by drawing humorous cartoons. The teacher remarked that students were exceptionally on task during the entire lesson. Students put forward consistent effort during the entire lesson—even students who couldn't sketch gave input to partners who did the drawings or wrote descriptions of what was happening in the cartoons. Students enjoyed using their artistic abilities to show their newly acquired knowledge of Earth science topics.

References

Duffy, S. A. 1999. Cartoon characters as tobacco warning labels. PhD diss., University of Illinois at Chicago.

Garner, R. L. 2006. Humor in pedagogy: How ha-ha can lead to aha! *College Teaching* 54 (1): 177–180.

National Research Council (NRC). 1996. *National science education standards.* Washington, DC: National Academies Press.

Rule, A. C., and J. Auge. 2005. Using humorous cartoons to teach mineral and rock concepts in sixth grade science class. *Journal of Geoscience Education* 53 (5): 575–585.

Rule, A. C., D. A. Sallis, and J. A. Donaldson. 2008. Humorous cartoons made by preservice teachers for teaching science concepts to elementary students: Process and product. Paper presented at the Annual Graduate Student Research Symposium, Cedar Falls, IA. (ERIC Document Reproduction ED no. 501244)

Song, Y., M. Heo, L. Krumenaker, and D. Tippins. 2008. Cartoons: An alternative learning assessment. *Science Scope* 31 (5): 16–21.

Yager, R. E. 2000. A vision for what science education should be like for the first 25 years of a new millennium. *School Science and Mathematics* 100 (6): 327–341.

Zhao, Y. 2008. What knowledge has the most worth? *School Administrator* 65 (2): 20–27.

Resources

Gwynne, F. 1982. *The sixteen hand horse.* New York: Bookthrift Company.

Gwynne, F. 1988. *A little pigeon toad.* New York: Simon and Schuster Books for Young Readers.

Gwynne, F. 2009. *A chocolate moose for dinner.* New York: Paw Prints.

Gwynne, F. 2009. *The king who rained.* New York: Paw Prints.

This article first appeared in the Summer 2009 issue of Science Scope.

Chapter 18

Cartoons

An Alternative Learning Assessment

by Youngjin Song, Misook Heo, Larry Krumenaker, and Deborah Tippins

Wait! Before you grab that comic book from some student's hands, maybe you should ask what that comic book does for the student that you haven't done. Perhaps you haven't tried to teach with some humorous cartoons? Nah, we all try that; many teachers are stand-up comedians in training. But have you thought about using cartoons and comics for assessing your students' science learning?

Science education reform documents in the United States, such as the *National Science Education Standards* (NRC 1996), envision that all students learn science with understanding. How do we, as science teachers, know that our students understand the science presented in the classroom? Our own teaching experience as well as research on science learning has provided evidence that assessment of student learning is much more than just giving paper-and-pencil

tests and grades. To fully understand student learning, science teachers need to know the ideas that students bring into the classroom. Plus, good assessment calls for ongoing evaluation of students' progress and difficulties with learning on an everyday basis.

This approach to assessment emphasizes the inclusion of alternatives to traditional paper-and-pencil evaluations, that is, "alternative assessments." By using these, science teachers can obtain information about students' strengths and weaknesses in science while the learning is taking place. Alternative assessments can include portfolios, journals, concept maps, oral interviews, and so on. Cartoons are one tool that has been used successfully as a means of assessing student learning in science (Perales-Palacios and Vilchez-Gonzalez 2005). They can be used at the beginning, middle, and end of a unit to assess students' prior knowledge and new learning. Recognizing the value of cartoons, we developed strategies for using them as an alternative assessment tool in middle school science.

We chose to use cartoons with a unit on force and motion because research has shown that students come into a physical science class with preconceived notions about the topics and have difficulties understanding these concepts (Wandersee, Mintzes, and Novak 1994). Alternative assessment strategies using cartoons can help science teachers assess students'

Further Reading

- "The Alchemy of Art: Transforming Student Art Into Science Knowledge in the Chemistry Room," from the January 2005 issue of *The Science Teacher* ideas, old and new, and difficulties they experience as they learn the force and motion concepts.

ASSESSING THE IDEAS STUDENTS BRING TO THE CLASSROOM

To assess what students already know about a specific concept, we use a "concept cartoon," a term first coined by Naylor and Keogh (1999) to refer to a cartoon-style format that includes competing views or explanations of a specific phenomenon. To develop a concept cartoon, the teacher selects a science concept for which they would like to know students' preexisting ideas. Then, the teacher draws or finds a cartoon that includes an everyday situation. To either of these, the teacher now adds several alternatives that depict students' common conceptual difficulties or confusions relevant to that concept. Teachers can decide what kinds of situations should be included in the cartoon based on their own experiences or the research literature. The cartoon should include three or more different ideas that students could have about the situation.

For example, Figure 1 is representative of a concept cartoon in our selected context. This cartoon illustrates the concept of inertia. When the cart hits the rock, the pig is supposed to keep moving in the same direction of the moving cart according to Newton's first law of motion, often referred to as the law of inertia. When a concept cartoon is used as a kind of pretest, students are given a copy of the artwork at the beginning of the lesson. Three or four students work together in a group and for a few minutes discuss each viewpoint represented in the cartoon until team members reach a consensus about a particular position. Once each group has arrived at a consensus, they take a minute to share the idea they have selected and explain their choice using a scientific rationale. After each group presentation, all students should be provided time to ask questions of the presenting team members.

Once this is complete, explain the scientific ideas contained in the cartoon to students. According to Newton's first law of motion, inertia is defined as the tendency of objects to resist changes in their state of

Figure 1

Concept cartoon

IMAGES COURTESY OF THE AUTHORS

motion; that is, an object in motion tends to stay in motion and an object at rest tends to stay at rest when no force is exerted on it. However, when students see this cartoon, different groups are likely to express different viewpoints based on their prior knowledge and preconceptions. Through the above process, students should become aware of their own ideas, practice justifying their claims, consider alternative explanations, and finally adopt the scientific concept. In addition, preparing the cartoon gives teachers the time to reflect on their own conceptions and become more familiar with common alternative conceptions students are likely to hold.

ASSESSING STUDENTS' PROGRESS AND DIFFICULTIES

Cartoons are especially effective in engaging students in scientific dialogue. Even the quietest students in class can be motivated to talk when a familiar cartoon character becomes the protagonist of their dialogue. Active dialogue facilitates student understanding of scientific concepts and also provides a context for teachers to recognize student progress and learning.

A second way of using cartoons is more open than the concept cartoon. In this approach, science teachers use a *cartoon cut,* that is, one extracted

Figure 2

Cartoon-project guide

The cartoon project is designed to apply scientific concepts to your everyday life. In this project you will create your own cartoon strip and story.

Procedure

1. Find a situation that contradicts the science concepts that you have learned. Your source can be anything that you can observe, such as a real-life situation, TV animations, favorite comic books, and so forth. Make sure you cite the source.
2. Bring that situation into the classroom by taking a picture of it, copying it, or drawing the scenario.
3. In your group, share and discuss your situation and find alternative situations that match with scientific conceptions.
4. Based on your group's discussion, make a cartoon strip with an interesting story as a group. You can either choose one particular situation and add more cuts or use all the situations that your group members bring and mix them. When you make a story, use the scientific terms that you have learned.
5. After making your cartoon strip, tape it to the wall. Then, write your opinion about the other groups' work based on two criteria: scientific plausibility and interest of the ideas.

image selected from a cartoon strip, comic book, TV animation, or other similar artwork. In order to have students articulate their thinking about a specific concept, teachers present a cartoon cut that contains a situation in which one or more scientific concepts are applied or misapplied (see Resources for suggestions). The difference between a concept cartoon and a cartoon cut is that a cartoon cut does not provide alternative viewpoints about a specific science concept within the cartoon. Rather, students have to find a "hidden" science concept. Furthermore, each group has to come up with its own scientific explanation about the situation instead of supporting one established viewpoint.

For example, many middle school students are likely to be familiar with the Warner Bros. animations of Road Runner and Wile E. Coyote. In the animation, the Coyote often falls faster than other objects so that he gets into trouble when hit by other falling objects. Students who understand free-fall motion in relation to Newton's second law can argue that the situation is nonscientific because all free-falling objects, which are falling under the sole influence of gravity, fall with the same acceleration regardless of their mass.

This example can be used to assess student learning while the concept of free fall is being taught. After having students watch a six-minute animation of Road Runner and Wile E. Coyote (see Resources for samples), the teacher can provide the cartoon cut or ask students to reflect on a situation that contradicts the scientific concepts illustrated in the film clip. Then, students can develop scientific claims and list evidence to argue for and support their ideas. In such contexts, the teacher has the opportunity to ascertain students' levels of understanding in relation to the concept, and students have the opportunity to reflect on their own understanding and practice communicating their scientific ideas.

One of the advantages of using a cartoon cut, especially one familiar to middle school students, is that it is effective in motivating ongoing discussion. The cartoon cut can provide teachers with information about where students are located in their learning and how the unit should progress. Furthermore, the cartoon cut can be used to assess how well students observe, gather facts, and then hypothesize which "laws of nature" are found in this cartoon universe, and how they may or may not differ from ours.

ASSESSING STUDENTS' APPLICATION OF SCIENCE TO EVERYDAY LIFE

Cartoons can also be used to assess students' learning outcomes and their abilities to apply a science concept to everyday situations. We developed a cartoon project that provides students with an opportunity to draw cartoon strips and create stories. Figure 2 illustrates a sample cartoon project guide. Teachers may adapt it to any science unit. The situation, which should contradict one of the science concepts students have learned, can come from their lives or other cartoons such as TV animations, favorite comic books, and so forth. However, the actual situation must violate the principles underlying the concept. Students are asked to bring the situation to class by taking or copying a picture, or drawing the scenario. In the classroom, students share their examples in small groups, discuss the situations, find plausible alternative situations, and finally make a cartoon strip and write an underlying story that corrects the flawed science of the original situation. All students' cartoon strips are exhibited, and their peers are asked to write an opinion about each cartoon strip in terms of the scientific plausibility and interest of the ideas. Each student's peer evaluation is useful as a supplemental means to further understand the writer's level of understanding. The entire process is assessed by a summative assessment rubric.

Figure 3 illustrates an actual sample that was drawn by a group of students as part of a cartoon project in a force-and-motion unit. Students found the situation in a TV animation in which two animals (the pursuer and the pursued) suddenly stopped on the edge of a cliff. Students thought that this situation contradicted the law of inertia since the animals could not stop immediately. Therefore, they drew a cartoon strip in which two animals fell down rather than halted, with a humorous ending.

Figure 3

Students' sample work

Figure 4

Rubric for a cartoon project

	Outstanding	Good	Needs More Work
Cartoon Strip and Story			
Use of scientific terms	Student often and correctly uses scientific vocabulary.	Student correctly uses a couple of scientific terms.	Student never uses or misuses scientific terms.
Understanding of Newton's laws of motion	Student shows evidence of clearly understanding Newton's laws of motion.	Student shows evidence of partially understanding Newton's laws of motion.	Student shows little evidence of understanding Newton's laws of motion.
Writing skill	Student organizes the story well and explains the situation clearly.	Student explains the situation clearly.	Student misses some parts necessary for the communication of the story.
Completeness	Student elaborates the drawing and finishes it.	Student creates a story but does not finish the drawing.	Student does not finish the drawing or the story.
Creativity	Student's ideas are sophisticated, humorous, and original.	Student's ideas are humorous and original.	Student's ideas are not original.
Peer Evaluation			
Completeness	Student completes all the other groups' evaluations.	Student completes all but one or two groups' evaluations.	Student completes evaluations for less than half the groups.
Use of criteria	Student evaluates peers' products in terms of scientific plausibility and interest to others.	Student evaluates in terms of scientific plausibility.	Student evaluates in terms of interest to others or based only on the drawings.

In addition, the rubric in Figure 4 can be used to evaluate the entire process of a cartoon project in a force-and-motion unit and include such elements as assessing students' ideas about force-and-motion concepts, the completeness of their work, and their creativity. Each student's written story can also be used as a supplemental assessment to further understand the student's conceptions. Teachers can modify this rubric for any science unit.

ASSESSMENT

Using cartoons as a summative assessment tool in the project is effective in many aspects. First, it is relevant to students' interests. Second, it promotes students' skills of observation, establishment of hypotheses, and inductive thinking. Third, it enhances students' abilities to apply scientific knowledge to their real lives. (Who can deny that TV animations and comic books are a part of children's lives?) Fourth, it stimulates students' curiosity, creativity, and desire to express themselves by having their ideas represented in the form of interesting drawings and comic stories. Finally, it offers an opportunity for teachers to assess student understanding in an authentic way.

CONCLUDING THOUGHTS

We have introduced three ways of using cartoons as an alternative assessment tool in middle school science classrooms: assessing students' prior conceptions, students' progress and difficulties with learning, and students' learning outcomes. The use of cartoons in a middle school fits several characteristics of young adolescents (Forte and Schurr 1993). They are curious about the world around them, so they need varied situations for exploration. Young middle school students are more likely to be agents of their learning if they can use a familiar medium. Active learning activities are preferred over passive ones so hands-on learning experiences are necessary. Students also need opportunities to express their creativity.

Cartoon strategies for assessment are useful for teachers as well. Students' abilities to discuss, draw, and write their own cartoons provide science teachers with a more complete picture of how their students understand scientific ideas. Besides assessment, these approaches can function as a powerful learning tool for students to interpret and synthesize scientific knowledge and to apply what they know. Using cartoons is much more exciting than simply providing facts. Though our examples involve a force and motion unit, we feel sure other areas of science can be assessed in this same way.

Copyright Concerns

Even if it doesn't explicitly say so, every creative work, including cartoons, is copyrighted. This doesn't mean, though, that you can look but not touch. Guidelines for "fair use" in educational venues are found in the U.S. Copyright Office's *Circular 21*, "Reproduction of Copyrighted Works by Educators and Librarians" (*www.copyright.gov/circs/circ21.pdf*).

Briefly, teachers may make multiple copies for classroom use. No more than one copy per student. Usage must be at the "instance and inspiration of a single teacher" and when the time frame doesn't allow enough time for asking permission. Use it only for one course in the school and do this kind of copying no more than nine instances per class, per term (current news publications such as newspapers can be used more often). "Consumables" can't be copied. Don't use the cartoon every term; if you plan to, write for permission before your next usage. Higher authority cannot compel you to use it. Copying can't be a substitute for buying the original resource, and you can only make copies from legally acquired originals.

As for video clips, teachers may use these materials in the classroom without restrictions of length, percentage, or multiple use. The material must be legitimately acquired (a legal copy). It must be used in a classroom or similar place "dedicated to face-to-face instruction" and is not for use as entertainment or reward. The use should be instructional. The place should be a nonprofit educational institution. You should check with your own local media committee for its policies as well.

Students have slightly more liberal guidelines than teachers; they may incorporate portions of copyrighted materials when producing projects for specific courses. The usage limits for them are no more than 5 images from one artist, and no more than 10% or 15 images from a collection, whichever is less. So if a student photocopies a cartoon from one of his or her books to show you, it's apparently OK. Students must cite their sources.

Some of the above information is derived from the Library Services copyright page at the University of Maryland University College (*www.umuc.edu/library/copy.shtml*).

Finally, there is no prohibition on displaying the original illustration in front of the class, on a document camera, Elmo, or opaque projector and adding your alternative choices for the cartoon cut on your own separate paper, blackboard, or PowerPoint slide. And nothing stops you from taking inspiration and doing your own cartoons with your own characters.

—*Larry Krumenaker*

References

Forte, I., and S. Schurr. 1993. *The definitive middle school guide: A handbook for success.* Nashville, TN: Incentive Publications.

National Research Council (NRC). 1996. *National science education standards.* Washington, DC: National Academies Press.

Naylor, S., and B. Keogh. 1999. Constructivism in classroom: Theory and practice. *Journal of Science Teacher Education* 10 (2): 93–106.

Perales-Palacios, F. J., and J. M. Vilchez-Gonzalez. 2005. The teaching of physics and cartoons: Can they be interrelated in secondary education? *International Journal of Science Education* 27 (14): 1647–70.

Wandersee, J., J. Mintzes, and J. Novak. 1994. Research on alternative conceptions in science. In *Handbook of research on science teaching and learning,* ed. D. L. Gabel. New York: Macmillan.

Resources

Cary, S. 2004. *Going graphic: Comics at work in the multilingual classroom.* Portsmouth, NH: Heinemann.

Gonick, L. 1991. *The cartoon guide to physics.* New York: HarperCollins.

Internet Resources

Concept Cartoons
www.conceptcartoons.com/index_flash.html

Conceptual Physics
www.conceptualphysics.com

Video clips featuring Wile E. Coyote
www.youtube.com (Search for Wile E. Coyote.)

This article originally appeared in the January 2008 issue of Science Scope.

Chapter 19

Science Newsletters

by Melissa Nail

Having students write and publish their own newsletters is a great way to integrate reading and writing, infuse technology, and build home-school relationships. These newsletters can be used to keep parents informed of what is being taught in class, important test dates, homework and project due dates, and any other information you'd like to share. Involving students in the creation of the newsletters increases their feeling of ownership and reduces the chances that the newsletter will end up in a wastebasket or forgotten in a locker.

GETTING STARTED

My students write their articles using Microsoft Word and lay out the newsletter using Microsoft Publisher. Publisher, which is included in the Microsoft Office suite of programs, is very helpful because it provides a Newsletter Wizard tool that walks students through the steps of setting up a newsletter. All you really need, however, is some kind of word processing software. Today's software allows you to set up columns, place text, import images, and change the type and size of fonts to create a very attractive newsletter. Your students are probably already familiar with how to set up and use word processing software, but you should allow time for a review of the basics. Before they can create their newsletters, students will need to know how to open, edit, and save documents within the word processing program. They will also need to know how to copy and paste text and place graphics in their documents.

PUTTING IT ALL TOGETHER

Once students are familiar with the software, the focus can turn to the content. To get things started, I ask students to brainstorm topics for articles. If they need some guidance, I suggest a few topics, such as explanations of content studied in class, reports on class activities, or summaries of experiments. Topics also can include reminders about upcoming holidays and school closings; reports on new equipment, animals, or other resources in the classroom; and news about

Further Reading

- "Classroom Newsletter," from the February 2005 issue of *The Science Teacher*
- "Extra! Extra! Learn All About It," from the November 2007 issue of *Science Scope*

Figure 1

Sample student newsletter

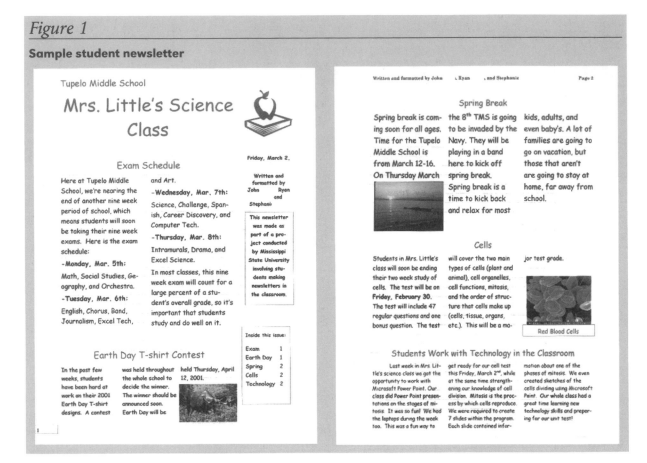

the science club, field trips, or after-school events. I contribute a piece to each newsletter called "Teacher's Corner." I distribute it electronically and each group incorporates the column into its layout. I use this column to communicate with parents regarding dates of exams, topics for home study, requests for parent speakers or presenters, and suggestions of ways parents can participate in their child's education.

The internet is the primary source of graphics used to accompany the articles, but students can also create their own figures and illustrations using drawing tools included with the word processing software or other programs. Inexpensive collections of images on disk can also be found at your local computer or electronics store. If a scanner is available, students can also scan in images they have drawn freehand or found in books or magazines. When a particularly good graphic related to a topic is identified or created, such as a student's illustration of a plant cell drawn using Paint Brush, students are encouraged to share it with the other groups.

There are a number of options available to classroom teachers for putting together the student-created newsletters. If wireless laptops are available in the school, the teacher can simply check out the laptop cart for this

project. If the school has a computer lab, the classroom teacher can schedule the lab for the creation of the newsletters. The newsletters can also be created in classrooms with only one or two computers available. This option might require more planning and more time because the students would have to alternate and rotate use of the available computers, with only one group at a time publishing a newsletter while other class members work on other exercises. Some schools now have classroom sets of PDAs that teachers can check out and use. If this is the case, students could use the PDAs to individually input their articles using a program such as Word to Go, Hot Sync the PDA with a desktop computer, and quickly and easily insert the individual articles into their group's newsletter. Some teachers may also wish to collaborate with colleagues within the school so that the students are writing the articles during a language arts lesson and putting together the newsletters during a technology or computer lesson.

In most cases, a cooperative team of students can create a two-page newsletter in only three class sessions. One session is used for brainstorming, planning, and initial prewriting activities. The second session is used for writing and editing articles, and the third session is used for final editing and inserting the articles into a newsletter template. The most time-consuming part of the process seems to be finding appropriate graphics. Selecting one member of each team to be responsible for illustrations or compiling a shared library of appropriate illustrations seems to be a beneficial strategy for speeding up the production process. Another time-saver (especially as students are initially learning to produce their own newsletters) is for the teacher to either create or designate a particular newsletter template to be used.

Each group's newsletter is printed on the school's printer and duplicated on the school copier to make a copy for each member of the group. Unfortunately, our budget did not allow for each student to get a color copy of the newsletter. However, students can take the original file home and print their own color copies if they have access to the necessary software and hardware. The file can also be e-mailed home for students and parents to view in color onscreen. Many students will have their own personal e-mail addresses you can

use. Permission should be obtained in advance, however, before you collect and use any parent's e-mail address. Before making copies of the newsletter for distribution, I review the content of each one. This usually takes me about a day.

FINAL PAGE

The student newsletter project proved to be very successful. Students are actively involved in the publication of the newsletters, displaying more excitement for writing articles than they had ever demonstrated for merely writing reports on topics studied. When the finished newsletters are distributed each quarter, students receive them excitedly. They show off their finished products to classmates, then carefully put the newsletters in folders and book bags to take home and share with their families.

This article first appeared in the Summer 2005 issue of Science Scope.

The Use of Stations to Develop Inquiry Skills and Content for Rock Hounds

by William R. Veal and Anna T. Chandler

Teaching the rock cycle can overwhelm even the most enthusiastic rock hound. As middle school science teachers, we constantly struggle with an appropriate balance between Earth system content and experiential activities. We have found that stations can be successfully employed to teach rock cycle content while reinforcing development of inquiry skills. Using stations, teachers are able to implement the abundance of available activities that incorporate content, standards, and inquiry skills.

With an increased focus on state testing and accountability, many middle school educators feel as if it's essentially impossible to cover the amount of content, with quality instruction, in the specified time period. We can all learn from some sound pedagogy often used in elementary and early childhood classrooms (Powell 2005). Stations, or centers, have long been used in elementary classrooms to introduce

Further Reading

- "The Station Approach: How to Teach With Limited Resources," from the February 2007 issue of *Science Scope*

concepts, develop student motor and process skills, and promote inquiry learning. Middle school teachers can implement stations to develop inquiry skills through investigating questions, designing and conducting experiments, and drawing conclusions.

A station is a student-centered activity that is located in a certain area of the classroom in which a student, alone or in a small group, learns content through a hands-on activity (Tomlinson 1999). Stations typically consist of readings, videos, graphic organizers, activities, demonstrations, and experiments. When designing stations, the emphasis needs to be on the interaction of students with content in an inquiry manner. A station should include laminated directions and safety guidelines, supplies, and background content information.

With proper planning, the stations should represent art, literature, reading across the content area, data collection, data interpretation, and experiment development. For example, developing a process for determining mineral content of a rock allows students to think, develop, test, and explore content through a hands-on, tactile activity. By using a multitude of station types, teachers can target all learning modalities. Teachers can modify existing text-based and internet-based lessons and activities and generate their own ideas based upon their experiences and the needs of students. Steps for station development are as follows:

- Determine the standard to be covered.
- Search for existing activities and lesson plans, based upon the standard, that incorporate the inquiry skills mentioned above.
- Prepare the directions to reflect individual or group work.
- Gather other necessary components of the station (consumables, handouts, background information, technology, and manipulatives).

STATION DEVELOPMENT AND IMPLEMENTATION

The context for our development of stations occurred in an eighth-grade science classroom in which students were learning about types of rocks and the rock cycle. The development of our stations took a large amount of time initially, but once established the stations were completed over a four-day period and easily stored for the next year. Identifying the activities, collecting the materials, and organizing the individual stations consumed most of the planning time. Existing laboratories, demonstrations, and worksheets are among the many teaching tools that we modified to create station activities.

Because the stations were student centered, well-written and descriptive directions that allow students to proceed independently were essential. Directions should be made durable through the use of permanent markers, page protectors, and laminations and secured by taping them to the work area. When applicable, the directions should include safety guidelines. Additional copies of directions should be readily available in the event that one gets marked up or taken away.

Each station contained a set of questions, a graphic organizer, or a short worksheet, which all students had to complete. Figure 2 lists the stations we developed, gives the inquiry skills learned, and offers a description of each station. We spread the stations throughout the classroom to limit the noise and confusion. On the first day of the stations, we showed proper skills to be used, briefly explained each station's directions and safety procedures, and provided models of completed work where appropriate. Students used their lab books to record their work and responses and demonstrate their level of understanding. To avoid an accumulation of students at one station, we developed more stations than there were groups of students. Our students were required to finish all stations; however, teachers can

Figure 1

National Science Education Standards Content Standard (NRC 1996)

As a result of activities in grades 5–8, all students should develop the following:

Science as Inquiry
- Abilities necessary to do scientific inquiry
- Understanding about scientific inquiry

Earth and Space Science
- Structure of the Earth system

differentiate learning by requiring some students to complete additional stations of varying complexity.

During the days of the stations, we restocked consumables for each class period, monitored student understanding, and made sure students cleaned their work areas. This can easily be accomplished with a checklist for each station that includes supplies, clean-up tasks, and a diagram or picture of the station arrangement.

The most effective stations were well planned, clear and concise, easy to complete, hands-on, student centered, and inquiry based. They allowed for critical thinking and provided a certain amount of freedom, while also promoting small-group communication. Stations that were not successful were knowledge based and centered on content dissemination, and had students follow a linear set of directions.

Classroom management is integral to the success of the stations. We established procedures on the first day. On subsequent days, organized chaos filled the classroom, but students understood the expectations. This amount of activity in the classroom heightened student engagement.

STATION ASSESSMENT

We used a combination of alternative, authentic, and traditional assessment methods to evaluate student learning. Traditional methods of graded work included worksheets, graphic organizers, and traditional open-ended questions to reinforce content at each station. An authentic assessment method, a summative interview, assessed students' content knowledge while reflecting the interactive and collaborative nature of the stations. In addition, the interview questions focused on the abilities and understandings of inquiry skills. Individual interviews were conducted while other students completed an independent written assessment. A rubric was used (Figure 3, p. 98)

Figure 2

Rock stations and inquiry skills

Station Name	Inquiry Skill	Description
Minerals in rocks	• Design and conduct a scientific investigation • Use scientific tools safely and accurately • Analyze data • Communicate results	• Students are given the following materials: hammer, goggles, plastic bag, microscope, slide, minerals-in-granite identification sheet. • Students create and carry out a step-by-step plan to isolate and identify the minerals in granite. They discuss and explain how granite is broken down in nature.
Sand to sandstone	• Make observations • Develop a hypothesis • Use appropriate measurement skills	• Students compare and contrast sand and sandstone. They discuss how they can create sandstone with sand and how this occurs in nature. Students follow a recipe from FOSS Earth History Kit to make sandstone.
Igneous rock formation	• Make predictions • Draw conclusions	• Students predict what will happen when the sugar cube is exposed to extreme heat. The teacher leads a group demonstration by melting sugar cubes ("sedimentary rock") using a skillet and a hot plate. • Students observe the "lava" as it cools and hardens to form "igneous rock."
Fossil observation	• Interpret data • Draw conclusions	• Students observe and identify fossils found in sedimentary rock and determine the process in which the animals and plants were captured in the rock.
Metamorphic rock formation	• Make models • Make observations	• Students take three balls of different-color play dough and make a snowman-shape figure. They press down on the snowman and use a plastic knife to cut the play dough in half. Students observe the cross-section, which resembles a foliated metamorphic rock.
Rock identification	• Make observations • Collect and organize data • Interpret and develop a dichotomous key	• Students collect data on physical properties (hardness, color, streak, magnetism) and chemical properties (reaction to acid) of three rocks. Students create a dichotomous key.
Content reading	• Organize information	• Students read a passage in their text and complete a graphic organizer that compares the three types of rocks based on their physical and chemical properties.
Videos	• Make connections • Draw conclusions	• Students view a video on classroom computers and answer teacher-created questions.
Folding study guide	• Organize information	• Students create a folding study guide to group characteristics of the three types of rocks.

chapter 20

to grade students' understanding of the formation of sedimentary, metamorphic, and igneous rocks and how they are interrelated in the rock cycle. A benefit from completing an inquiry, hands-on, minds-on, and visual activity at a station was the experiential nature. The experiential learning was supported when students, reflecting on their work or answering questions on a test, often looked in the direction of the stations to help them visualize different rock types and recall the rock formation process. Many students referred to different stations and the skills they completed at the stations when answering questions about the rock formation. One student wrote in her station reflection, "I think the stations helped me learn this information better because if I'm stuck on a question, I can think back to when we did the stations." Her statement reflects the interactive and experiential nature of stations.

REFLECTION

While stations contextualize content for students, they also provide a format to effectively incorporate science content and inquiry skills. Stations are a pedagogical solution to time constraints that so many educators face. Stations are not just one-shot activities; they are specific standards-based activities that contain durable materials that can be easily stored and maintained for use in subsequent years. With all of the activities and demonstrations that we traditionally use to teach specific concepts, the development of stations was easy to implement. Stations are valuable because they use a limited set of materials in which groups of students cycle through, using the resources one group at a time. Stations allow the time to focus on more than one concept, while providing individual students with the time needed to complete activities, discuss content, and answer higher-order questions. We designed stations to help students make connections, transfer knowledge, and see relationships. For example, students completed the rock cycle by simulating the weathering of rocks (minerals in rocks station), the cementation of sediments (sand to sandstone station), the melting of sedimentary rocks and formation of igneous rocks (igneous rock formation station), and the formation of metamorphic rocks (metamorphic rock formation station).

Figure 3

Rock interview rubric

15 points	• Describe that a metamorphic rock is one rock changing to another by two of the following processes: heat, pressure, time. • Describe that sedimentary rock is created from sediments and two of the following processes: precipitation, compaction, cementation. • Describe that igneous rock is formed by magma and lava cooling and hardening. • Describe how one rock can become another through the rock cycle. • Show an in-depth understanding of how the rocks relate to one another.
10 points	• Describe one process involved in the formation of each type of rock. • Show a basic understanding of how the rocks relate to each other.
5 points	• Show some understanding of the above information. • Convey partial understanding of rock types.

Directions for a written quiz:
• Describe the formation of igneous, sedimentary, and metamorphic rocks.
• Describe how the three types of rocks are related in the rock cycle.

References

Powell, S. D. 2005. *Introduction to middle school.* Upper Saddle River, NJ: Pearson, Merrill Prentice Hall.

Tomlinson, C. A. 1999. *The differentiated classroom: Responding to the needs of all learners.* Alexandria, VA: Association for Supervision and Curriculum Development.

This article first appeared in the September 2008 issue of Science Scope.

Chapter 21

Examining Current Events in Science, Mathematics, and Technology

by John Eichinger

OVERVIEW

The national standards in science and mathematics call for these subjects to be taught from personal and social perspectives, thus strengthening students' decision-making skills. Preeminent science educator Paul DeHart Hurd called for "a curriculum that relates science to human affairs, the quality of life, and social progress" (1994, p. 109). In this activity students examine news coverage not only from the perspective of science, technology, and math, but also based on the story's impact on real people, that is, implications for human rights and social justice. Interdisciplinary connections are embedded in an engaging, accessible, and human context, as students read, analyze, and openly discuss a teacher-selected news article. By facilitating honest dialogue, the teacher helps students confidently face controversial topics and develop crucial critical-thinking skills.

PROCESSES/SKILLS

- Describing
- Analyzing
- Concluding
- Inferring
- Inquiring
- Communicating

RECOMMENDED FOR

Grades 5–8: Individual, small-group, or whole-class instruction
By choosing news articles appropriate to students' ages and ability levels, this activity can be adjusted for any student in these grades.

TIME REQUIRED

1–2 hours

Further Reading

- "Up-to-the-Minute Meteorology," from the February 2004 issue of *Science Scope*
- "Word Wall," from the February 2006 issue of *The Science Teacher*
- "Digital Field Trips," from the February 2004 issue of *Science Scope*

MATERIALS REQUIRED FOR MAIN ACTIVITY

- Enough photocopies of a news article for the entire class (consider newspaper, magazine, and internet sources)

CONNECTING TO THE STANDARDS

NSES
Grade 5–8 Content Standards:
Standard A: Science as Inquiry
- Abilities necessary to do scientific inquiry (especially using appropriate tools to gather data, thinking critically, and considering alternative explanations)

Standard E: Science and Technology
- Understanding about science and technology (especially that perfectly designed technological solutions do not exist)

Standard G: History and Nature of Science
- Nature of science (especially that thorough evaluation and interpretation of investigations is a crucial part of scientific inquiry)

NCTM
Standards for Grades 3–8:
- Communication (especially analyzing and evaluating the mathematical thinking of others)
- Connections (especially recognizing the connections among mathematical ideas and to investigations outside mathematics)

SAFETY CONSIDERATIONS

Basic classroom safety practices apply. If students use online sources, be certain to monitor student web use to avoid contact with inappropriate sites and information.

ACTIVITY OBJECTIVES

In this activity, students

- read and analyze a current event not only for its content in science, technology, or math, but also for its human impact, including human rights and social justice implications.

MAIN ACTIVITY, STEP-BY-STEP PROCEDURES

1. Begin by choosing a current event article from a newspaper, news magazine, or the internet. The article should be directly relevant to some aspect of science, technology, or math. Because real-world issues seldom fall conveniently under a single subject heading, your article is likely to have indirect connections to other fields. Your choice of current events could raise issues and questions related to history, sociology, psychology, or politics. Be sure to exercise sensitivity to school district policies and community perspectives when choosing a news item. As you make your choice of articles, you might also consider the human rights issues associated with the news event. Such issues are not beyond the scope of the elementary or middle school classroom and are, in fact, highly motivating for students due to the relevance of the topics and the opportunities for authentic dialogue. Take into account the human rights issues associated with news stories regarding global climate change, immunization, cloning, colonization of other planets, organ transplants, environmental hazards, health care, or waste management. An integrated analysis of the news article, including consideration of human rights issues, is promoted by Activity Sheet 1, page 102.

2. Photocopy the article for all class members and read it together, clarifying new concepts and terms as necessary. Have students break into small groups for analysis of the article, with each individual student recording responses on Activity Sheet 1. Facilitate the analysis by moving around the room from group to group, listening, asking, and assessing.

3. Resume whole-class instruction by discussing the groups' results and reactions to the article. Throughout the analysis and discussion, prompt students to notice and express their personal responses to the article. Encourage an awareness and use of authentic student voice, keeping in mind that this activity is designed to illuminate student perspectives via intellectual exploration, not simply to generate standardized, right/wrong responses. Personalize the discussion, especially at the elementary level; for example, ask, "How might a young person like you react to these conditions?" Ask students to consider the article's impact on various demographic groups.

   A basic approach to this analysis and discussion is as follows:

   a. Clarify the problem. What is going on? Broaden students' understanding of the situation.
   b. Define the basic pro and con reactions to the article, concentrating on science, math, and technology connections.
   c. Consider the human rights implications: violations, infringements, advancements.

Who is affected by the situation, and how are they affected?

d. Through open dialogue, determine workable solutions to the problem. Determine areas of impasse.

e. What must be done to implement the solution(s)?

f. What additional information is needed to help solve the problem?

The teacher has a number of responsibilities in this activity: to help students understand that every problem may not have a simple answer; to help students learn to accept an element of uncertainty; to seek fairness in presenting and discussing the topic; to avoid proselytization and the tendency to oversimplify complex topics; and ultimately to induce authentic, critical thought.

DISCUSSION QUESTIONS

Ask students the following:

1. Do all situations in real life have simple solutions? Explain your answer.

2. When faced with a complex problem, is it a good idea to consider more than one perspective before making any decisions? Explain your answer.

3. What types of careers might involve solving complex problems?

ASSESSMENT

Suggestions for specific ways to assess student understanding are provided in parentheses.

1. Were students able to summarize the chosen article? (Use student responses to Activity Sheet 1 as performance assessment and observations made during Procedure 3 as embedded evidence.)

2. Could students explain the importance of the article in terms of its science, technology, or math content? (Use student responses to Activity Sheet 1 as performance assessment and observations made during Procedure 3 as embedded evidence.)

3. Were students able to discuss the human rights aspects of the current event? (Use observations made during Procedure 3 as embedded evidence.)

4. Did students, through open dialogue, arrive at solutions to the problem, or could they explain

Sample Rubric Using These Assessment Options

	Achievement Level		
	Developing 1	Proficient 2	Exemplary 3
Were students able to summarize the chosen article?	Attempted unsuccessfully to summarize the article	Summarized the article in a general way	Successfully summarized the article, including details and varying viewpoints
Could students explain the importance of the article in terms of its science, technology, or math (STEM) content?	Attempted unsuccessfully to explain the importance of STEM content	Generally explained the importance of STEM content	Explained the importance of STEM content in detail, noting interdisciplinary connections
Were students able to discuss the human rights aspects of the current event?	Attempted unsuccessfully to consider the article's human rights aspects	Generally considered the article's human rights aspects	Discussed the article's human rights aspects in detail, including viewpoints of different people
Did students, through open dialogue, arrive at solutions to the problem, or could they explain why a solution is not yet feasible?	Attempted unsuccessfully to arrive at a solution to the problem presented	Successfully described a solution to the problem presented	Successfully described several solutions to the problem or explained why solutions are not yet fully feasible

why a solution is not yet feasible? (Use observations made during Procedure 3 and student responses to the Discussion Questions as embedded evidence.)

OTHER OPTIONS AND EXTENSIONS

1. Students, either individually or in groups, might wish to expand their knowledge about the news topic. Encourage them to present their research to the class in the form of a debate, play, poem, video, or art project.
2. Have students write letters related to the news report. They should address the letters to parties in or related to the current event article *and actually send them*. Be judicious about sharing your own perspective so that your students will more readily develop and record their own views. This exercise is especially empowering when the news issue is local and students can see the results of their correspondence.
3. Have students explore news sources for relevant articles of their own choosing. Let them present and discuss those articles in groups or in a classwide forum.

Reference

Hurd, P. D. 1994. New minds for a new age: Prologue to modernizing the science curriculum. *Science Education* 78 (1): 103–116.

Resources

Jennings, T. E., and J. Eichinger. 1999. Science education and human rights: Explorations into critical social consciousness and postmodern science instruction. *International Journal of Educational Reform* 8 (1): 37–44.

LeBeau, S. 1997. Newspaper mathematics. *Teaching Children Mathematics* 3 (5): 240–241.

McLaren, P. 1995. *Critical pedagogy and predatory culture: Oppositional politics in a postmodern era*. New York: Routledge.

O'Connell, S. R. 1995. Newspapers: Connecting the mathematics classroom to the world. *Teaching Children Mathematics* 1 (5): 268–274.

Activity Sheet 1

Examining current events in science, technology, and mathematics

Respond to the following based on the news article from class.

1. Summarize the article in 30 to 50 words. List any new words that you don't understand.

2. What does the article have to do with science, technology, or math?

3. Who might be affected by the situation or problem reported in the article? How might they be affected?

4. Why is the article important? (Consider the viewpoints of several different people.)

5. What additional information is needed to resolve the problem reported in the article?

Silbey, R. 1999. What is in the daily news? *Teaching Children Mathematics* 5 (7): 390–394.

This chapter first appeared in Activities Linking Science With Math, 5–8 *(2009), by John Eichinger.*

PART 4

Instructional Lessons
That Maximize
the Science Budget

Chapter 22

Forensics on a Shoestring Budget

by Joseph A. Greco

In recent years, forensic science has gained popularity thanks in part to high-profile court cases and television programs. Although the cost of forensic equipment and supplies may initially seem too expensive for the typical high school classroom, I developed an activity that incorporates forensics into my 10th-grade biology curriculum while staying within budget.

The activity involves estimating a time of death based on fictitious police and medical examiner reports. Students review the documented evidence of a crime and compare it to known forensic information. This activity requires no elaborate equipment or supplies and my students were challenged to apply their knowledge using inquiry.

Further Reading

- "How Many Lefties in Our Classroom?" from the September 2008 issue of *Science Scope*
- "Science of Skin Color," from the November 2007 issue of *Science Scope*

GETTING STARTED

First, the teacher develops a scenario—a fictitious crime complete with police and medical examiner reports (Figure 1). This activity is focused on estimating time of death, so to develop a good scenario, all of the physical evidence collected should match up within a couple of hours. The information provided in both the police and medical reports must coincide.

To develop the scenario, teachers must review general background information on forensic science. The book *Crime Scene: The Ultimate Guide to Forensic Science* (Platt 2003) devotes an entire section to how time of death is determined. With help from this book, teachers can develop fictitious documented material to assist students in determining the relative time of death for the victim.

The evidence may include

- when the victim was last seen,
- how the body was found (e.g., position, physical abnormalities),
- contents of the stomach and small intestine,
- body temperature,
- appearance of the body (e.g., discoloration of skin, stiffness of extremities), and

- appearance of the eyes (e.g., ocular cloudiness).

Students then take this data and compare it to known forensic information about time of death such as

- reduction rate of body temperature after death (*algor mortis*),

- time it takes to move food through the digestive tract, and
- length of time for postmortem conditions to set in (*rigor mortis* or *livor mortis*).

Once students have cross-checked all the evidence with the known data, they can then estimate the time of death and support their claims.

Figure 1

Sample laboratory scenario

As a junior crime scene investigator, one of your duties is to assist your supervisor with estimating the time of death for a recent victim in the area. Your supervisor has left you with a copy of both the police and medical examiner reports and requests that you use the documents and your knowledge of forensics to determine when the victim died. Once time of death is established, your supervisor would like your professional opinion on whether the victim's death was an accident or a murder. Take your time and conduct a comprehensive analysis.

Police Report

The body of John Doe was found at 145 Maple Avenue at around 6:00 a.m. on Friday, November 12.

Appearance of the body: The victim was lying face up at the bottom of the basement stairs and appears to have died of injuries sustained from a fall (massive contusion to back of head and broken neck). The body temperature of the victim at 7:00 a.m. was approximately 32.6°C. His eyes were open and covered with a cloudy film. The victim had purple marks on the front of his neck and chest consistent with lividity.

Appearance of the surroundings: A pizza box was found on the kitchen table from Pizza House along with a

receipt saying that it was sent out for delivery Thursday, November 11, at 6:00 p.m. There was no evidence of forced entry, but the back door to the home was left unlocked.

Supplemental information: Michael Deer, a good friend of the victim, found the body of the victim at 6:00 a.m. on November 12. He claimed to have come over to pick up the victim for work and entered through the back door when the victim did not come out to the car. Deer said that he had eaten pizza and watched football with the victim the night before, and the victim was still alive when Deer left the house at 11:00 p.m.

Medical Examiner's Report

The male victim is approximately 177 cm tall and weighs 67 kg. The cause of death appears to be blunt force trauma to the back of the skull and a broken neck. Both of these injuries are consistent with a fall down stairs. There was pizza located in the victim's stomach, but none had entered the small intestine.

Known Forensic Information

Body temperature (algor mortis): The body temperature drops about 0.4°C every hour after death. This is an average measurement and may be faster or slower depending on the victim's size, what the victim was wearing, and the

environmental temperature where the victim was found.

Ocular film: If the victim dies with his or her eyes open, a thin cloudy film forms over the lenses in less than three hours.

Skin tone (lividity): After death, the blood stops flowing and settles to the lowest points of the body due to gravity. After about six hours, the skin will develop purple or red marks where the blood has pooled.

Digestive system: Food moves completely through the digestive tract in about 32 hours. After the food reaches the stomach, it takes about three hours before it moves to the small intestine. Once in the small intestine, it takes food about five more hours before it reaches the large intestine.

Questions

- Based on the evidence, when do you think the victim died?
- How did the multiple forms of evidence help to pinpoint the time of death of the victim? (Show your work.)
- Do you believe Mr. Deer's account that the victim was alive at 11:00 p.m.?
- Was the body moved after death? How would you know?
- Do you think the victim's death was an accident or a murder? Why?

TIME OF DEATH

One common piece of data for estimating time of death is body temperature. On average, body temperature drops about 0.4°C per hour after death, a process called *algor mortis*.

To estimate time of death, students can use this information to form a graph of body temperature in relation to time. Depending on the students' learning level, the teacher may either provide this forensic information or have students research it independently. In either case, students compare the provided police and medical reports to the known forensic information to estimate when the crime took place. Body temperature is a great way to incorporate graphing skills, but additional forms of evidence allow students to estimate the time of death with greater accuracy and encourage more investigation.

Additional evidence may include information about lividity. Lividity, or *livor mortis*, results after the blood in the body stops flowing and starts to settle out to the lowest parts of the body turning the skin purple or red. This process takes about six hours to complete. In the police report, the teacher can say whether or not the police officer noticed any skin discoloration and where on the body lividity marks were found.

Lividity evidence can help the scenario in two ways. First, it allows a general estimation of time of death (i.e., more or less than six hours). Second, because gravity always causes the blood to settle to the lower parts of the body, lividity allows the crime scene investigator (the student) to determine whether or not the victim's body was moved after death. If a body was moved, there is a greater chance that the victim's death was a murder rather than an accident. The more evidence (e.g., stomach contents, *rigor mortis*, decomposition) the teacher adds, the more complex the activity becomes for students.

FURTHER REFINEMENT

As students become more comfortable with the analysis of data, the teacher may want to throw in some contradictory facts that allow students to question the reliability of the collected evidence (Figure 1). For example, the scientific data may suggest that the victim died around 9:00 p.m., but an eyewitness reported he had seen the victim around 11:00 p.m. Students initially recheck their own calculations, but if they are confident with their data analysis, they may want to dismiss the eyewitness's claim and consider him a suspect.

Depending on the skill of the students and the creativity of the instructor, many scientific lessons can be tied in whether teachers choose to stay as simple as body temperature or increase the complexity to include blood typing and DNA analysis.

Reference

Platt, R. 2003. *Crime scene: The ultimate guide to forensic science.* New York: Dorling Kindersley Publishing.

This article first appeared in the Summer 2005 issue of The Science Teacher.

Chapter 23

Making Mendel's Model Manageable

by Karen Mesmer

G enetics is often a fascinating but difficult subject for middle level students. They can see
the results of genes in every organism, but
trying to visualize what happens at the level of genes
is challenging for concrete thinkers. This activity
presents an approach that helps students understand
how genotypes can translate into phenotypes. In this
lesson, based on the article "Gummi Bear Genetics"
(Baker and Thomas 1998), students examine gummi
bears and see whether they can determine the geno-
type for color in three generations of a bear family. Students need to be introduced to the concept
of dominant and recessive genes before this activity.
Using gummi bears and gummi dolphins gives students an opportunity to solve problems using Mendel's model and then to revise the model when the
data do not fit.

Further Reading

- "Toothpick Chromosomes: Simple Mani-
  pulatives to Help Students Understand
  Genetics," from the April 2003 issue of
  Science Scope

GUMMI GENETICS

For the first part of the activity, you will need 43
gummi bears for each group of students in your classroom. The cost for this lab is $15 or less depending
on the type of gummi bear that is used. I usually have
students work in groups of three, with eight groups
per class of 24 students. I use red gummi bears for
the dominant color and clear for the recessive color,
but any two colors can be used. The gummi bears for
each generation of the bear family are put in a small
sealable plastic bag labeled with marker as "Parents,"
"Kids," or "Grandkids." (See Figure 1, p. 110, for exact
numbers for each family.) The three small bags are
put in a large sealable plastic bag labeled as "Family
A," Family B," or "Family C." I also use a marker to label
the back of each gummi bear as male (M) or female (F).
I cover the label with clear tape so that it isn't rubbed
off during the lab. This also keeps students from eat-
ing the gummi bears.

To begin this two-day activity, each group selects
the bag of gummi bears for Family A. Following the
activity sheet, students fill out the number of male
and female bears of each color for each generation
(see Activity Sheet 1, p. 112). Then they find the
ratio of the most common color of bear to the least
common. They see, for example, that in Family A,

the parents are red and clear, but the kids are all red. Students can then deduce, from their previous study of dominant and recessive genes, that red is the dominant color in gummi bears and that clear is recessive. Filling in a Punnett square for each cross (generation 1 to make generation 2, and generation 2 to make generation 3) confirms their solution. It is evidence that the students have solved the problem if the color that they assign to each bear fits correctly in the Punnett square. To gather additional evidence, they need to complete the chart and Punnett squares for Family B and then Family C.

REVISING THE MODEL

Models are often revised in science. If data are found that do not fit an existing model, the model can be added to or changed, or a new model can be developed to replace or coexist with the current model. I use gummi dolphins (or another gummi creature) for the second part of this lab to illustrate codominance.

This lab is set up the same way as the gummi bear lab except that you need 65 dolphins for each group and five different families (see Figure 2). Each generation goes in a small sealable plastic bag and then is put in a larger "family" bag. There will be five families per group and students should only work on one family at a time. I allow them to trade for another family only when they have finished the previous one.

A red dolphin and a yellow dolphin have orange offspring. Students record the same data that they did with the gummi bears and try to determine the inheritance pattern (see Activity Sheet 2, p. 113). They see

that it does not fit Mendel's model of simple dominance, because with parents that are two different colors there are three different colors of offspring instead of only two.

A "scientific symposium" convenes at the end of the lab. Students share their ideas about the inheritance patterns in the color of gummi dolphins and critique each other's views based on the data. I have

Figure 1

Bear Families

FAMILY A:
(R,R) crossed with (r,r)
Parents: 1 red male, 1 clear female
Kids: 7 red (3 males, 4 females)
Grandkids: 6 red (3 males, 3 females), 2 clear (1 male, 1 female)

FAMILY B:
(R,r) crossed with (R,r)
Parents: 2 red (1 male, 1 female)
Kids: 7 red (4 males, 3 females), 2 clear (1 male, 1 female)
Grandkids (from a clear female kid and a red male kid): 5 red (2 males, 3 females), 2 clear (2 females)

FAMILY C:
(r,r) crossed with (r,r)
Parents: 2 clear (1 male, 1 female)
Kids: 4 clear (3 males, 1 female)
Grandkids: 6 clear (2 males, 4 females)

Figure 2

Dolphin families

FAMILY A:
Parents: 1 red male, 1 yellow female
Kids: 4 orange (2 males, 2 females)
Grandkids: 2 red (1 male, 1 female), 4 orange (3 males, 1 female), 2 yellow (2 females)

FAMILY B:
Parents: 1 yellow male, 1 yellow female
Kids: 3 yellow (1 male, 2 females)
Grandkids: 5 yellow (3 males, 2 females)

FAMILY C:
Parents: 1 red male, 1 red female
Kids: 5 red (2 males, 3 females)
Grandkids: 4 red (2 males, 2 females)

FAMILY D:
Parents: 1 orange male, 1 yellow female
Kids: 4 orange (3 males, 1 female), 4 yellow (2 males, 2 females)
Grandkids (from an orange male kid and a yellow female kid): 3 orange (2 males, 1 female), 3 yellow (1 male, 2 females)

FAMILY E:
Parents: 1 orange male, 1 red female
Kids: 3 red (2 males, 1 female), 3 orange (1 male, 2 females)
Grandkids (from a red male kid and an orange female kid): 3 red (2 males, 1 female), 3 orange (2 males, 1 female)

each group present its ideas and the evidence that supports them. Most groups come up with the idea that the two colors blend to get a mix of the colors. We then try to come to consensus as a class as to what is the best idea that takes into account all the data, is realistic, and can be used to make predictions. I make sure students know the current understanding of codominant traits, which is that they produce offspring that are in between the two parents; for example, red and yellow parents produce orange offspring.

CONCLUSION

Research on using modeling suggests that it is an effective approach that provides a framework for students to use both to understand science concepts and to solve problems (Cartier and Stewart 2000). Developing a model gives students a sense of how science works and how data translate into scientific ideas. Being able to use a model to solve novel problems and then to develop a new model to explain anomalous data helps students understand each model better and experience the way real scientists do inquiry. This set of activities takes into account the concrete thinking skills of many middle school students, helping them grasp an abstract idea such as classical genetics.

References

Baker, W., and C. Thomas. 1998. Gummy bear genetics. *The Science Teacher* 65 (8): 25–27.

Cartier, J., and J. Stewart. 2000. Teaching the nature of inquiry: Further development in a high school genetics curriculum. *Science and Education* 9: 247–61.

This article first appeared in the March 2006 issue of Science Scope.

Activity Sheet 1

Gummi genetics

Procedure

1. Working with your group, get a large bear family bag containing three smaller bags with the gummi bear generations inside. The smaller bags are labeled "Parents," "Kids," and "Grandkids."
2. Empty the contents of only the Parents bag onto the table and record the colors on the chart below. An "M" on the back of the bear indicates that the bear is male. Put the gummi bears back in the bag. These two bears mated to produce the offspring in the Kids bag.

Data chart

Family_____

	Number of red	Number of clear	Ratio of most common color to least common
Parents	Male = Female =	Male = Female =	
Kids	Male = Female =	Male = Female =	
Grandkids	Male = Female =	Male = Female =	

3. Empty the contents of only the Kids bag onto the table and record the colors on the chart. Put the gummi bears back in the bag. A male and female kid produced the offspring in the Grandkids bag.
4. Empty the contents of only the Grandkids bag onto the table and record the colors on the chart. Put the gummi bears back in the bag.
5. Draw a pedigree for the three generations of the Family you have. Color in any circle or square that has (R, R) genes. Put a dot in the middle of those that are (R, r). Leave blank those that are (r, r).
6. Fill in the Punnett squares below to show how it would be possible to get the results that you did from the family you worked with.

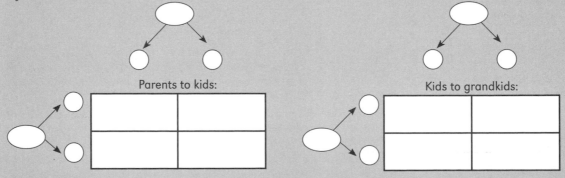

Parents to kids:

Kids to grandkids:

7. Draw a pedigree for the three generations of this bear family.
8. Repeat the procedure (copying a new data chart for each) for the other two bear families.

NATIONAL SCIENCE TEACHERS ASSOCIATION

Activity Sheet 2

Gummi dolphins

Procedure

1. Working with your group, get a large dolphin family bag. It will have three small bags of gummi dolphins inside. The smaller bags are labeled "Parents," "Kids," and "Grandkids."
2. Empty the contents of only the Parents bag onto the table and record the colors on the chart. An "M" on the back of the dolphin indicates that the dolphin is male. Put the gummi dolphins back in the bag. These two dolphins mated to produce the offspring in the Kids bag.
3. Empty the contents of only the Kids bag onto the table and record the colors on the chart. An "M" on the back of the dolphin indicates that the dolphin is male. Put the gummi dolphins back in the bag. A Male and Female kid mated and produced the offspring in the Grandkids bag.
4. Empty the contents of only the Grandkids bag onto the table and record the colors on the chart. Put the gummi dolphins back in the bag.

Data chart

Family_____

	Number of red	Number of clear	Ratio of most common color to least common
Parents	Male = Female =	Male = Female =	
Kids	Male = Female =	Male = Female =	
Grandkids	Male = Female =	Male = Female =	

5. Draw a pedigree for the three generations of the Family you have. Color in any circle or square that has (R, R) genes. Put a dot in the middle of those that are (R, r). Leave blank those that are (r, r).
6. Fill in the Punnett squares below to show how it would be possible to get the results that you did from the family you worked with.

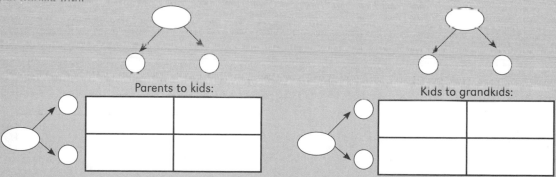

Parents to kids:

Kids to grandkids:

7. Draw a pedigree for the three generations of this dolphin family.
8. Repeat the procedure (copying a new data chart for each) for the four other dolphin families.

Chapter 24

Lighten Up Your Lesson
Matter, Optics, and Bubbles

by Jeffrey S. Maxwell, Beixin Julie He, Wendy deProphetis, and J. Aura Gimm

Have you ever taken the time to really think about a soap bubble? If not, we think you are in for a fun-filled surprise. Soap bubbles can be used to teach scientific principles such as phases of matter and the reflection of light. The study of soap bubbles addresses the National Science Education Standards for grades 5–8 related to the properties and changes of properties in matter (NRC 1996).

SOAP BUBBLES MATTER

As we all know, a soap bubble is filled with air, but how should a bubble's shell be classified? In other words, is a soap bubble's shell made of a liquid, a solid, or something else entirely? Begin with a class discussion on this topic to really get your students thinking about what makes a liquid a liquid and a solid a solid. Have them brainstorm ideas and guide them with such questions as, "What do rocks, metals, and other solid objects all have in common?" Write down their observations on a chart for everyone to see. This discussion should lead your students to notice many different traits of matter, such as the fact that solids maintain a definite size and shape. The reason that solids maintain their size and shape is that the particles in a solid are tightly packed together and are not free to move. The particles in a liquid are not as tightly packed together as the particles in a solid. Although they maintain a definite size, liquids take on the shape of any container into which they are poured.

After discussing the basic properties of liquids and solids with your students, have some volunteers blow bubbles around the classroom while everyone answers the bubble observation questions (see Figure 1, p. 116). A bubble maker such as one of the Gazillion Bubble products (*www.funrise.com*) can produce large quantities of bubbles. However, a variety of less expensive bubble solutions come equipped with wands and also work well. Students can also use varying sizes of wands to see the effect of wand size on bubble shape and color. To avoid a mess, this activity can be performed outside, or you may wish to place newspapers on the floor to prevent slippery spills. One benefit to performing this activity indoors is that, after wiping down the classroom, all of the desktops are clean! Be sure to have your students wear

Further Reading

- "Bubble Shapes," from the March 2003 issue of *Science and Children* safety chemical-splash goggles as bubble solution can be an eye irritant.

In the context of the previous discussion and the students' observations, talk about the specific nature of soap bubbles with your students. In particular, focus on the soapy shell that surrounds the internal pocket of air. Ask students whether they believe that the shell is a liquid, a solid, or something else. For example, in a liquid, molecules are free to change orientation and position. It might, therefore, be tempting to say that a soap bubble is a liquid because moving swirling patterns cover its surface, it comes from a liquid solution, and it feels wet (and pops!) when you touch it. On the other hand, it might be tempting to say that a soap bubble is a solid. Unlike liquids, solids maintain a definite shape because their molecules are fixed in terms of both position and orientation. For example, a pearl will maintain its shape without any outside help. In contrast, if you want a liquid to hold the same shape as a pearl, you must either freeze it or pour it into a round container. Consistent with solids and in contrast to liquids, a soap bubble possesses a definite shape of its own—in this case, a sphere. Write down the reasons for and against each idea as a class.

REVEALING THE TRUTH

In actuality, a soap bubble cannot properly be classified as either a liquid or a solid. Rather, it belongs to a unique and extremely important, often-neglected phase of matter known as liquid crystal. Although the notion may seem paradoxical, the term *liquid crystal* itself is really quite informative. For example, when we ask students what they think is meant by liquid crystal, we almost always get one or more of the following answers: a crystal that is made out of liquid, a liquid that is made out of crystals, a liquid-like crystal, or a crystal-like liquid. However, after providing one of these answers, students often appear puzzled. How can something be both liquid-like and crystal-like at the same time?

The answer resides in the fact that the intermolecular forces in liquid crystals are both weak enough to allow flexibility of molecular movement (liquids) and strong enough to lend a degree of structural order (solids). In other words, the molecules in a liquid crystal are free to move around (translate), but must maintain a common orientation with respect to their neighbors. This possession of fluid-like properties by a structurally ordered substance has lead scientists to classify liquid crystal as a unique state of matter that exists somewhere between a liquid and a solid (Collins 1990).

Students can research the answer to this and many other questions, such as, "What are the current applications for liquid crystals?" and "What are potential future applications for liquid crystals?" (see Internet Resources). Additionally, consider having students research today's practical applications of liquid crystal technology, including the development of advanced polymers and the production of flat-screen televisions and display panels for computers, digital cameras, cellular phones, iPods, and similar devices. You may also be familiar with liquid crystals in the form of mood rings, thermometers, and paints that change color as a function of heat. In such products, we are able to observe nanoscale alterations in a liquid crystal's

---

Figure 1

Bubble observation questions

1. What do the soap bubbles look like? Size? Shape? Other characteristics?
2. How do the bubbles behave? What do they do when they are first blown? Just before they pop? While they are floating or sitting still?
3. Consider a bubble's outer shell—the soapy film that creates the bubble. How is it like a liquid? How is it like a solid? How is it different from liquids and solids? What is it after it pops?

Figure 2

Color observation questions

Look at the soap bubbles near a window or other good source of light. View them from several different angles and pay careful attention to the rainbow patterns and colored bands that cover each bubble's surface.

1. Which colors do you see? Are there any colors missing?
2. Why do you think soap bubbles reflect these different colors?
3. Which colors are brightest when the bubbles are first blown?
4. Which colors still remain just before the bubbles pop?
5. Why do you think the colors change with bubble thickness?
6. Do different regions reflect different colors? If so, why?
7. Pick a single point on a bubble's surface. Does it stay the same color when you view it from different angles? If not, why do you think this is the case?

Take-home questions

1. What is the definition of *iridescence*?
2. Can you provide examples of iridescent phenomena found in our everyday lives?

---

underlying molecular structure by discerning perceptible color changes with the naked eye. Scientists are currently exploiting the unique color-changing properties of liquid crystals in the form of chemical and biological sensors that have been specially tuned to respond to particular agents. Additionally, biology is filled with examples of liquid crystalline materials, including such macromolecules as proteins, lipids, and deoxyribonucleic acid (DNA). In fact, the unique combination of structural order and fluidity that is present in liquid crystals is integral to life as we know it.

IRIDESCENCE

In addition to introducing the exciting world of liquid crystals, soap bubbles serve as a fun and familiar example of iridescence. While volunteers blow bubbles again, have students answer the color observation questions (see Figure 2). The iridescent colors that decorate a soap-bubble's surface illustrate the fact that sunlight consists of all the colors of the rainbow. Additionally, this colorful display can be used to teach about light wave interference.

Incoming light reflects off both the inner and outer surfaces of a bubble's soapy shell. These reflected light waves, in turn, either sum together (constructively interfere) or cancel one another out (destructively interfere). The net degree to which reflected light waves constructively or destructively interfere is determined, in part, by a bubble's thickness. If a given wavelength is reflected off the inner and outer surfaces of a bubble's shell in phase with itself or another wavelength of visible light, it will constructively interfere and produce brilliant color. In contrast, light waves that are reflected out of phase will destructively interfere and result in muted or absent color.

Again, consider having students research the examples of iridescent phenomena that appear all around us (see Internet Resources). For instance, iridescence can be observed in cloud formations and oil slicks. It can also be seen in butterfly wings, peacock feathers, beetle shells, certain types of algae, and the interior of seashells. Perhaps most strikingly, as noted by Isaac Newton, subtle changes in viewing angle can drastically alter which, if any, colors appear on an iridescent surface. Try it! One intriguing hypothesis about biological iridescent surfaces, such as beetle shells and butterfly wings, is that they function to help animals evade potential predators by creating visual confusion (Platt 1996).

ADDITIONAL NOTES AND RESOURCES

Both of these exercises can be flexible in terms of time and complexity. For example, you may choose to devote additional time to teaching about the molecular structure of liquid crystals, electromagnetic radiation, and the visible spectrum. You may also incorporate this activity into review sessions concerning the different states of matter or the fundamentals of optics. Additionally, instead of purchasing a commercial brand of bubble solution, you can easily and inexpensively make your own (see Internet Resources). This is especially useful if you plan to combine these exercises with additional bubble activities or generate human-size bubbles.

ACKNOWLEDGMENTS

Funding was provided by the National Science Foundation through the Interdisciplinary Education Group of the Materials Research Science and Engineering Center (DMR-0079983) and the Internships in Public Science Education program (DMR-0120897) at the University of Wisconsin–Madison. We would also like to thank Greta Zenner, Professor Wendy Crone, and the staff of Discovery World Museum in Milwaukee, Wisconsin.

References

Collins, P. J. 1990. *Liquid crystals: Nature's delicate phase of matter.* Princeton, NJ: Princeton University Press.

National Resource Council (NRC). 1996. *National science education standards.* Washington, DC: National Academies Press.

Newton, I. 1704. *Opticks: Or, a treatise of the reflexions, refractions, inflexions and colours of light. Also two treatises of the species and magnitude of curvilinear figures.* London: Printers to the Royal Society.

Platt, M. E. 1996. Iridescence in insects. *LORE Magazine.*

Internet Resources

About Liquid Crystals
   www.lci.kent.edu/lc.html
Bubblesphere
   http://bubbles.org
History and Properties of Liquid Crystals
   http://nobelprize.org/physics/educational/liquid_crystals/history/index.html
Iridescence in Nature
   www.mbari.org/staff/conn/botany/reds/iridaea/iridesc.htm,
   www.meteoros.de/iris/irise.htm

This article first appeared in the March 2006 issue of Science Scope.

Chapter 25

Shampoo, Soy Sauce, and the Prince's Pendant

Density for Middle-Level Students

by Meera Chandrasekhar and Rebecca Litherland

Which one could you carry more easily: 10 kg of Styrofoam peanuts or 10 kg of steel? Does the word *heavy* conjure images of thick syrup or a weighty suitcase? These common questions can lead to student misconceptions regarding mass and density. It is no wonder that students find density conceptually difficult.

In this article we describe a series of activities we have used with middle-level students. The first set of lessons explores density through the layering of liquids. In the second set we use some of the same liquids to explore the density of solids. The third set investigates how temperature affects the density of materials—primarily liquids. The fourth set leads to quantitative measurement of the density of solids. Concept development, problem solving, design, measurement, and quantitative activities are interwoven throughout these lessons. Each set of lessons is designed to conform to one full cycle of the 5E learning model (see Figure 1, p. 120 for an explanation and

Further Reading

- "Layered Liquids," from *Activities Linking Science With Math, 5-8* (2009)

timeline). Ideally these lessons should be done in order, but teachers may choose one or two for their classes as appropriate. The activities within each lesson, however, need to be done in order.

LESSON 1—LAYERING LIQUIDS

The introductory activity, Let's Make Layers, uses four liquids, provided in 2–4 oz. squirt bottles—soy sauce, shampoo (use a clear kind), corn syrup, and corn oil (see Figure 2, p. 121 for a complete materials list, including costs). A few drops of red and green food coloring are added to the shampoo and corn syrup, respectively, so the clear liquids can be easily identified. You may label the bottles, if you wish. These liquids are easy to use in a classroom since they are cheap and safe and do not mix easily. Shampoo helps with cleanup, too. Classroom management is easier if you store the liquids in small squirt bottles and allow each group to have a set of four bottles. Each group requires six plastic vials (see Figure 2). If you have several sections of a class in a single day, have at least two class sets of materials, so that the first set can be used, washed, and allowed to dry while the second set is being used.

Student groups are given the vials and two steps made of half-inch-thick wood blocks. Alternatively, you could use small books of the same thickness. Students are challenged to design a series of tests using the materials provided and to test liquids two at a time to sequence the liquids from the "lightest" to the "heaviest." Most groups decide first to choose two specific liquids, predict the order in which they will layer, and then layer them in a clear plastic vial. They then predict and layer all combinations of the liquids, two at a time, (for a total of six vials, see Figure 3, p. 122). Questions such as "Which liquid is always a top layer?" and "Which liquid is always a bottom layer?" guide students in sequencing the liquids. The students use the steps to place only those vials where the top layer of the vial placed on the bottom step is the same as the bottom layer of the vial placed on the step above it (see Figure 3).

This activity provokes several intriguing questions. Students frequently discuss whether the layering will be affected by the order in which they squirt the liquids (it isn't). Students often predict that shampoo will layer below soy sauce because it is more "gooey"— while in fact, soy sauce is "heavier" and layers below

shampoo. This discrepant event leads to a discussion of how "gooey" is not equivalent to "heavy." Layering is controlled by density, while viscosity governs the ease of flow of a liquid and is a property that does not directly relate to density. Of course, the temptation to layer all four liquids is too much to resist, but have students save that activity for the end, after they have layered the liquids in pairs.

Having experienced layering of dissimilar liquids, students are now ready for a more fine-tuned experiment, namely, the classic activity Layering Salt Solutions (see Resource). Students are once again challenged to order a set of salt solutions "from lightest to heaviest," using the same wood block steps. Salt solutions of four different concentrations are provided (typically one, two, three, and four tablespoons of kosher or pickling salt to one cup of water). Each solution is colored using a few drops of different food coloring. Students must now use care while making layers because salt solutions mix easily—it helps to use a medicine dropper, hold the vial at an angle, and add the second liquid drop by drop onto the side of the vial so it can slide

Figure 1

Learning cycle connections and timeline

Step	Purpose of Step
Engage (E1)	Students make connections between past and present learning experiences; their interest is excited.
Explore (E2)	Students manipulate materials to actively explore concepts, processes, or skills.
Explain (E3)	This step focuses students' attention on previous activities, provides opportunities to develop explanations or hypotheses, and introduces formal labels or definitions.
Elaborate (E4)	This step extends conceptual understanding, makes connections to related concepts, and applies students' understandings to the world around them
Evaluate (E5)	This step encourages students to assess understanding and abilities; the teacher evaluates their learning.

Lesson 1 **Layering Liquids** **(2 class periods)**	Lesson 2 **Liquids and Solids** **(2 class periods)**	Lesson 3 **Temperature Effects** **(1–2 class periods)**	Lesson 4 **Density of Solids** **(1 class period)**
Let's Make Layers: E1, E2	Egg and Saltwater: E1, E2, E3	Density Ball: E1, E2	Which Wood for a Raft?: E1, E2, E3
Working definition of density questions: E3	Box That Barely Floats: E5	Homemade Galileo Thermometer: E2, E3	Prince's Pendant: E4, E5
Layering Salt Solutions: E3, E4		Homemade Galileo Thermometer, expanded activities: E4, E5	
Layering Salt Solutions, quantitative: E4, E5			

Figure 2

Materials for activities

Let's Make Layers (Lesson 1)
(per group)
- 6 small plastic vials (3-dram, clear polystyrene, about $22 for case of 144; www.usplastic.com)
- 4 liquids in squirt bottles: shampoo (red), soy sauce (dark brown), corn syrup (green), cooking oil (pale yellow) (2 or 4 oz. size, with either flip top or dispensing cap; available from Delta Education or wholesale lab suppliers such as United States Plastic; about $.50 each.)
- Steps made with wood blocks (two 1.2 cm × 4 cm × 10 cm blocks)

Layering Salt Solutions (Lesson 1)
- 12 small plastic vials
- 4 medicine droppers (Reserve one for each color of solution.)
- 4 salt solutions, colored red, green, yellow, and blue
- Graduated cylinder
- Balance

Egg and Saltwater (Lesson 2)
(first four materials are used for the whole-class demonstration, then can be distributed to students)
- 5 beakers (each about 1 L in volume)
- Freshwater and four salt solutions
- 5 eggs
- Balance
- Graduated cylinder (100 ml or larger; per group)
- Overflow beaker to measure volume (per group)

Box That Barely Floats (Lesson 2)
(per group)
- Watertight plastic box (about 3–4 cm diameter and 3–4 cm tall, best with snap-on lid; can be purchased from craft stores or from plastic wholesalers; cost $0.30 to $0.50 each.)
- Fishing weights

- Ruler
- Modeling clay
- Electronic balance
- Overflow vessel to measure volume
- 5 gal. tub with water (one per classroom)

Density Ball (Lesson 3)
- Two 1 L beakers with hot and cold water
- Density ball (about $35–40, available from several science houses such as Boreal Labs, Science Source, and Ward's Science)

Homemade Galileo Thermometer (Lesson 3)
- 15 watertight plastic vials or 15 sealable, empty baby food jars
- Sand of different colors
- Gram balance, preferably with accuracy of 0.01 g

Which Wood for a Raft? (Lesson 4)
- Blocks of several different kinds of wood (from local lumber yard; cost varies with wood and cutting charges; four to six different varieties, with a total of about 12 blocks, are adequate for a class)
- Ruler
- Balance
- Calculator
- 5 gal. tub of water

Prince's Pendant (Lesson 4)
- Cylindrical rods of different metals (1.2 cm in diameter and about 5 cm long; available in sets from science suppliers; about $10–20 for a set of four rods; two sets per class)
- Prince's pendant
- Overflow beaker
- Balance
- Calculator
- 25 ml graduated cylinder

---

under the first layer if it must. Students are instructed to make two vials for each pair of liquids. Solution 2 is added after solution 1 in the first vial, and the order is reversed for the second vial.

In explaining the above experiments, students usually use the terms *heavier* and *lighter* rather than *denser*. At this early stage, it is acceptable for students to use everyday terms to describe the phenomena. We introduce the term *density* by asking all groups to write what they think the word conveys. Students are

asked to share their definitions in groups and to discuss questions they have as they compare definitions. Students often say dense means thick or heavy. They are asked to consider this their beginning definition of density, which they will refine as they continue with the activities.

Once students' ideas are discussed, a demonstration is used to provide a concrete example of the density of a salt solution. First students are asked, "Why is saltwater denser than freshwater anyway? If we add three tablespoons of salt to one cup of water, we have more mass, but we have more volume, too, right? Wrong. When salt dissolves in water, it gets into the spaces between water molecules, so it does not increase the volume, but it does increase the mass." An edible demonstration of this phenomenon is with a jar of jelly beans (representing water) into which we add two tablespoons of sugar. Shake it and the sugar "dissolves" into the crevices between jelly beans, but the volume of the mix remains the same. An extension of this demonstration is to see how many tablespoons of sugar you can add to the jar of jelly beans before it won't "dissolve" any more—a large-scale version of why solutions saturate.

Students are asked what data they could gather about the salt solutions that will provide a quantitative description of what *light* and *heavy* mean. Through class discussion of their experiments, students come to the conclusion that they can measure the mass and the volume of the salt solutions. Once these data are collected, students are asked how this information could be useful. Students are allowed time to brainstorm in groups and share ideas. Once students come up with the idea of dividing the mass of the salt solution by the volume, give students time to do the calculations with the data collected. They then discuss a possible formula for determining density and what that means.

The densities obtained by all groups in the class are collected on the board (or in a spreadsheet) and averaged. These values (and the salt solutions) are saved for a future activity.

To further develop the concept, questions that relate mass, density, and volume are used to guide additional discussion (Figure 4). These questions allow students to realize that for a specific object, such as a candy bar, when its volume (ml) decreases, its mass (g) decreases, but its density stays the same. Furthermore, the density of a specific material such as copper is the same regardless of its shape, mass, or volume. But to figure an object's density, we need to take the ratio of its mass to its volume. Thus, an object's density is given by the following expression:

$$density = \frac{mass\ of\ object}{volume\ of\ object}$$

Figure 3

Let's Make Layers

Six vials of layered liquids, in order from left to right: corn syrup and shampoo, oil and corn syrup, oil and soy sauce, shampoo and oil, shampoo and soy sauce, and soy sauce and corn syrup.

Vials of layered liquids are placed on wood block "steps," choosing only those vials where the top layer of a vial is the same as the bottom layer of the vial on the step above it. In other words, top and bottom layers in the vials line up horizontally.

Figure 4

Questions for a definition of density

1. Imagine a loaf of bread that is 10 in. long. If you place your palms flat on the slices and squeeze along the length so that the loaf becomes 7 in. long, what changes? Its length? Its mass? Its volume? Its density? Explain your reasoning.

2. A bungee cord is stretched to twice its length. What changes? Its mass? Its volume? Its density?

3. A candy bar is 10 cm × 2 cm × 4 cm. It has a mass of 120 g, and a density of 1.5 g/ml (1 ml = 1 cm³). You eat one quarter of the candy bar. What changes? Its length? Its mass? Its volume? Its density?

4. Two shoe boxes are identical in size. One contains beans and the other contains popcorn. What is the same and what is different? Mass? Volume? Density?

5. Which one is heavier—a pound of feathers or a pound of lead? Which one has more volume? More density?

6. Which is more dense—a stack of 5 pennies or a stack of 20 pennies? Explain your reasoning.

7. Besides shape, what is different between a 300 g rectangular block of copper and a 300 g round ball of copper? Mass? Volume? Density? Explain your reasoning.

LESSON 2—LIQUIDS AND SOLIDS

After investigating densities of liquids, students can now expand the concepts to solids in liquids. We begin this segment with Egg and Saltwater activities. We start with these questions: "What happens when we place an egg in a bowl of freshwater? A bowl of saltwater?" Students draw pictures of their predictions. After seeing the demonstration, they revise or redraw their pictures. Students frequently predict the results correctly—that the egg sinks in freshwater but floats in saltwater.

Next we ask, "What will happen if you place eggs in five solutions of saltwater of increasing density?" (Solutions are labeled A–E, with A being freshwater and E being saltwater of high density; the four salt solutions used in Layering Salt Solutions are reused.) Have students draw and label pictures of their predictions for each salt solution and record the actual results individually (see Figure 5). Ask student groups to make generalizations about how density affects when objects sink or float and then have students share the results.

Students usually think the solution density increases linearly across the vessels (it does), and they assume that the position of the egg must change linearly, too. However, floating and sinking do not obey the law of proportions. When the density of the egg is more than that of the solution, the egg sinks and stays at the bottom. When the egg is less dense than the solution, it floats (some part of the egg will touch or rise above the surface of the liquid). It is vital to point out that objects almost always either sink or float; they rarely "hang" between top or bottom surfaces.

Extend this activity by having students use the previously measured values of saltwater densities to predict the density of the egg. Students will frequently make the (correct) prediction that the density of the egg is more than that of salt solution C, but less than that of D. Students then find the density of the egg by using an overflow beaker to measure volume and a gram balance to measure mass.

Using an overflow beaker requires some skill. A discussion of possible errors (spillage, additional overflow if fingers are inserted along with the egg, the formation of a concave meniscus) allows students to distinguish between mistakes (made by the experimenter) and errors (due to inaccuracies inherent in the experiment). Data from all groups in the class are collected and students discuss outliers, then average acceptable data and compare it to their predictions. Owing to the common errors that creep into this exercise, using an all-class average of data is more useful. The density for the egg can now be compared to the predicted range.

The final activity in this lesson has students apply their understanding of density by merging their conceptual ideas about "how high" an object floats with their knowledge of the formula for density. In the Box That Barely Floats, students are given the challenge of designing a box that floats by just touching the surface of the liquid. They are given the following materials: a watertight plastic box, fishing weights, modeling clay, an overflow beaker, a ruler, and a balance (see Figure 2). Students must first decide how close the density of the box must be relative to that of water. Some students decide that 0.9 g/ml is adequate, while others choose 0.999 g/ml. They must then either measure or calculate the volume of the box and figure out the mass needed to achieve their chosen density. They then add weight to achieve the required mass. Students get to test the box only once, thus the design phase is critical. This activity makes students think

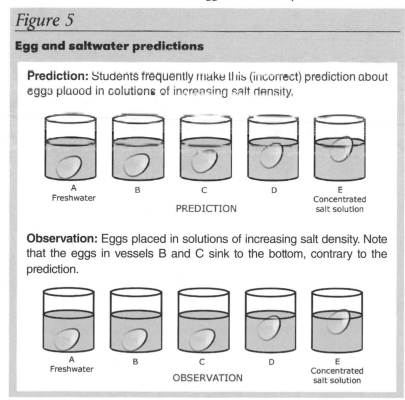

Figure 5

Egg and saltwater predictions

Prediction: Students frequently make this (incorrect) prediction about eggs placed in solutions of increasing salt density.

A Freshwater   B   C   D   E Concentrated salt solution

PREDICTION

Observation: Eggs placed in solutions of increasing salt density. Note that the eggs in vessels B and C sink to the bottom, contrary to the prediction.

A Freshwater   B   C   D   E Concentrated salt solution

OBSERVATION

conceptually, reflect about values and accuracy, apply the formula for density to design a device, make measurements, and finally, construct the device.

LESSON 3—TEMPERATURE EFFECTS

Usually at some point in the previous activities, students bring up questions about the relationship between temperature and density—sometimes triggered by a connection to hot air rising, as in hot-air balloons, or in relation to weather patterns. These student questions become the basis for introducing this set of activities. We begin with a discussion of the following questions:

- Your friend's little brother blows up a balloon and hides it in the refrigerator. What do you think the balloon will look like when he looks at it an hour later? How is it related to density?
- Why does smoke rise from a chimney?
- A house has heating vents on the floor in the bedroom and on the ceiling in the living room. Which room will be warmer in the winter? Explain your reasoning.

The Density Ball activity uses a device sold by several science suppliers. Ask students what will happen when the ball is dropped in a container of cold water and in a container of hot water, conduct the demonstration, and have students record observations and questions. Because the ball floats in cold water and sinks in hot water, students will correctly surmise that cold water is denser than hot water.

This demonstration is followed by the Homemade Galileo Thermometer activity where the class makes observations and takes data. The thermometers are made from baby food jars and colored sand, and require some skill to construct. Consider having honor students build the thermometers and saving them for future demonstrations. We made ours with 15 small baby food jars. The jars were cleaned, weighted with sand, sealed with a thin layer of petroleum jelly, and screwed tight. Alternatively, plastic vials with snap lids can be used. Our jars had masses between 107.0 and 105.4 g; however, these masses will vary with the jars used. It was useful to have a gram balance with an accuracy of 0.01 g in order to mass the jars accurately.

Because the density of pure water increases from 0.999 g/mL at 0°C to 1.000 g/ml at 4°C and then decreases to 0.972 g/ml at 80°C, the jars must be designed to have densities ranging from 0.99 to 0.985 g/ml to span a temperature range of 4 to 60°C. For the class demonstration, the jars are placed in a fish tank of warm water

(~60°C), and most of them sink. Ice is added and, as the water cools, the jars float to the surface one at a time. This demonstration takes about 30 minutes and is best started at the beginning of a class period and allowed to develop as the lesson progresses. Students are asked to work in groups to develop an explanation for what they observed, which is then shared with the class.

As an expansion or variation of this activity, students can first determine the density of premade jars through a mass/volume measurement. They then note the temperature at which each jar floats to the surface. Assuming that the water's density at that temperature equals that of the specific jar is an acceptable approximation. The class can then graph the jar density versus the temperature at which it floated up.

LESSON 4—DENSITY OF SOLIDS

Having experienced several aspects of density as it relates to liquids and solids, students can now proceed to examine the density of solids. So far students have primarily measured the mass and volume of salt solutions and eggs to determine density. In Which Wood for a Raft? students are introduced to other floating objects. The activity is set up as a challenge: A raft-building company wants to figure out which wood would be best for a raft. Students are supplied with blocks of different kinds of wood, each about 5–8 cm on each side (the blocks should be rectangular cut, not cubes, so they can float on the wide face). The class decides the criteria to be used. Most frequently students decide that the block that floats the highest (the one

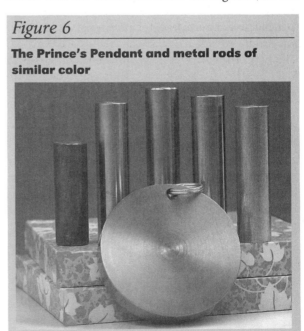

Figure 6

The Prince's Pendant and metal rods of similar color

with the lowest density) will make the best raft. Students find the volume from the geometry of the block (*volume = length × width × height*) and measure the mass and calculate the density of the wood. From this activity, students realize that different kinds of wood vary vastly in density. For example, the two extremes, cork and lignum vitae, are both used in industrial applications. Cork, with a density of 0.096 g/ml, comes from the bark of the cork oak tree that grows in Mediterranean countries. In contrast, lignum vitae, also known as ironwood, has a density of 1.3 g/ml, and comes from a tropical tree that grows in south Florida, Central America, and northern South America.

We suggest choosing four to six varieties of wood, with a range of densities. Be aware that blocks cut from different parts of a tree may have different densities. It is best to avoid knots in the wood, as they tend to make the blocks float unevenly. Students may research the properties of different woods and make connections to plant science, uses, or woodworking classes.

Most of the materials that students have encountered thus far float in either freshwater or saltwater. The next activity, the Prince's Pendant, introduces students to materials that are much denser than water. In our 21st-century version of the Archimedes story, the Prince of Agraba orders a pendant of titanium from a mail-order jewelry store. Suspicious of his delivery, he asks the class for assistance in determining whether the pendant is made of titanium, and if not, for an identification of the metal. The class is given the pendant (a disc 5 cm in diameter and 1 cm thick), and five rods of metal that have colors similar to that of the pendant (aluminum, lead, titanium, steel, and zinc/tin/nickel offer a wide range of densities, see Resource; see Figure 6). The rods are 1.2 cm in diameter and 5–8 cm tall. This diameter allows the rods to fit inside a 25 ml graduated cylinder, so that students can measure the volume of the rods by the displacement of a measured amount of water (several ml) in the graduated cylinder.

Students can measure the volume of the pendant using an overflow beaker, or they can calculate its volume. By comparing the density of the different metals to that of the pendant, students determine whether or not the pendant is made of titanium (it is not; titanium is expensive and hard to machine, so the pendant is made of steel).

CONCLUSION

These density activities are designed with relatively inexpensive materials. Students encounter densities of vastly different materials: wood (0.3 to 0.9 g/ml), metals (2.7 to 8.9 g/ml), salt solutions (1 to 1.06 g/ml), and water (1 to 0.96 g/ml). This aspect is often underappreciated—knowing ranges of possible values is almost more important than knowing exact values. Furthermore, students conduct measurements and repeatedly connect them to volume concepts learned in their math classes. They also measure volume using a variety of techniques. They use an overflow beaker, displace water in a graduated cylinder, and use geometric considerations for rectangular blocks and the cylindrical pendant. Students are repeatedly asked to interpret the meaning of their measurements.

The activities provide several connections to other areas of science and to everyday life. Students who have been to the beach have experienced the ease of swimming in saltwater as compared with freshwater. Those who live in cold climates have observed how water starts freezing over from the top of a lake or pond. The design of old-time boats and rafts depended closely on the choice of wood. And finally, all that shines is not titanium.

Resource

Barber, J. M. E. Buegler, L. Lowell, and C. Willard. 1988. *Discovering density.* Berkeley, CA: University of California, Berkeley.

This article first appeared in the October 2006 issue of Science Scope.

Chapter 26

Growth Potential

by Dana M. Barry

Students enjoy carrying out an exciting and challenging research project that combines science with computers and mathematics to investigate how polyacrylate animals change in size over time when placed in water and aqueous salt solutions. The hands on activity motivates students and provides them with the necessary skills and information to have enjoyable and rewarding science project experiences. Here they have an opportunity to solve a problem and to use the science process skills of observing, collecting, organizing, and analyzing data. Project results are displayed on individual posters, creatively prepared by the students. A schoolwide poster session is a great way to share the information and to build students' confidence and self-esteem.

In this activity, students determine how the percentage of NaCl (table salt) in an aqueous mixture affects the rate of water absorption (growth) by a polyacrylate animal. To start, each student is given a polyacrylate animal. These animals are molded models made of polyacrylate, a hydrophilic substance that attracts water molecules. They cost about $1 each and may be purchased at toy stores or from science supply catalogs. Use a variety of animal types and colors, but be certain to have four identical animals of each type—one for each of the four possible salt solutions in order to eliminate variables. I like to take a photo of each student holding his or her animal before we begin the project and again at the end so the difference can be observed; however, this is optional. Students then examine their animals, give them a name, and record their observations (length, mass, etc.) on a data table.

Provide each student with 500 ml of an aqueous salt solution (either 0, 1, 2, or 3% salt) in a large labeled container with a cover. Empty plastic food containers from school cafeterias work well. The 0% salt solution is pure tap water. The 1% salt solution has 5 g of salt per 500 ml of solution. The 2% salt solution has 10 g of salt per 500 ml of solution. The 3% salt solution has 15 g of salt per 500 ml of solution. The students are provided with these solutions and told the percentages in advance. Have them put the animals in their containers, cover and label them, and place them in a safe location. Containers may be stored in cabinets or on spacious countertops. For five consecutive days, students take daily measurements of the animals' length and mass, using metric rulers to determine length and a triple-beam balance with a 150 g capacity to measure mass. To do this, students open their containers and remove the animals from the salt solutions. Then they gently pat the animals with paper towels to remove excess water before taking measurements. Each student should wipe off any moisture on the balance after using it. When finished, the animals are put back in the containers, the covers are replaced, and the containers are returned to the storage shelf. After the last set of measurements has been made, take another photo of each student holding his or her animal.

Once the data gathering is complete, students prepare one graph showing elapsed time in hours versus length in centimeters and another graph showing elapsed time in hours versus mass in grams. These are then compared and discussed as a class. Students pair up with other students that have an animal of the same type and color, but of a different percent salt solution. They share data and graphs and compare results, and then draw conclusions about the effect of sodium chloride on the growth of their animals. Select pairs to orally share information about their animal experiment with the class.

The research results indicate that the more concentrated the salt solution, the less the increase of mass and length for each animal. This is because the salt hinders the water's ability to bond with the polyacrylate.

Additionally, students are expected to submit a short report of their research, which could include images and background information collected from the internet and library. Each report should include a description of what was done, the results, and concluding statements. Encourage students to creatively design individualized posters for their research projects. They can use their written reports, photos, data tables, graphs, polyacrylate animal pictures, and background information for the display. As an extension, students can obtain information about the real

---

Amazing Animals Activity

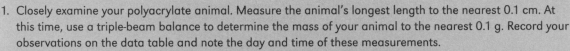

Materials (per student)
- 1 polyacrylate animal
- Metric ruler
- Triple-beam balance (150 g capacity)
- Assigned aqueous salt solution (either 0, 1, 2, or 3%) in a large plastic container with a top

1. Closely examine your polyacrylate animal. Measure the animal's longest length to the nearest 0.1 cm. At this time, use a triple-beam balance to determine the mass of your animal to the nearest 0.1 g. Record your observations on the data table and note the day and time of these measurements.
2. What do you think will happen to the animals in the different salt solutions?
3. Put your animal in 500 ml of the aqueous salt solution (either 0, 1, 2, or 3% salt as assigned). Write your name, animal type, color, and percent salt solution on the label. Then cover the container and place it in a safe location.
4. For the next four days, make daily measurements of length and mass (at approximately the same time each day). Before making measurements, gently pat the animal with a paper towel to remove excess water. Record your data on the table.
5. After the measurements are complete, prepare two graphs (either by hand or using a computer if available). One graph should include elapsed time in hours versus length in centimeters. The other graph should include elapsed time in hours versus mass in grams. Compare and discuss your results with the class.
6. Conduct research on your experiment and prepare a short report that includes a description of what was done, the results, concluding statements, photos, data table, graphs, animal pictures, and background information about the animal. Design a poster that displays your research to share with the class.

Student's name: _____ Animal color: _____

Animal type: _____ Concentration of the salt solution used: _____

	Time	Elapsed Hours	Length (cm)	Mass (g)
Day 1				
Day 2				
Day 3				
Day 4				
Day 5				

animals by using a search engine on the internet or encyclopedias in the library, listing at least one reference in their reports. Each student should prepare a three-page written report that includes a statement of the problem, a list of materials needed, a procedure to carry out the experiment, concluding statements, and references. The data table and two graphs are used to complement the written report. Students are assigned points for this activity, which culminates in the report and poster display. The project is worth 100 points, or the equivalent of a unit test grade. Students may receive points for including the title page, problem statement, list of materials, procedure, data table, graphs, concluding statements, references, and overall poster display (e.g., appearance and creativity).

This exciting activity provides students with a challenging research project that combines science with computers and mathematics. Students exercise problem-solving and critical-thinking skills as they investigate how polyacrylate animals change in size over time when placed in aqueous salt solutions. They also develop the technical skills of measuring and weighing. In addition, they prepare graphs, reports, and posters, and use the internet as a source of scientific information.

ACKNOWLEDGMENT

This research project was successfully carried out by students in Horizons 2002 and 2003, a special program for gifted seventh- and eighth-grade girls in New York State. It is a component of the Pipeline of Educational Programs offered at Clarkson University in Potsdam, New York.

This article first appeared in the April 2004 issue of Science Scope.

Chapter 27
Refraction of Sound

by Michael Horton

FOR THE TEACHER

This lab introduces students to refraction using something they can experience. They really do not understand what is going on when a pencil is put into water and appears to bend. It is difficult to see rays of light bending without the use of a laser or other expensive equipment. So for this first exposure to refraction, students use sound instead.

Postlab Answers

1. When sound travels from air through the CO_2-filled balloon, it gets focused. When sound travels from air through the helium balloon, it gets spread apart.
2. A hydrogen-filled balloon would spread the sound even more because it is even less dense than helium.
3. No. If you are in the water, the sound will simply bend, but not focus because the surface of the water is flat. Although sounds are different underwater, it is not because of this effect.

FOR THE STUDENT

Question

How does sound bend as it passes from one medium to another? How can this be used as a model of how light acts?

Safety

Dispose of any popped balloon parts immediately after the lab.

Materials

Helium balloon, empty balloon, glass or plastic soda bottle, vinegar (~125 ml), baking soda (~50 ml)

Procedure

When light travels from one medium (material) to another medium with a different index of refraction, the light bends. This property can be used to focus light rays or spread them apart. The same thing happens with sound, but it is the density of the mediums that must be different.

1. Obtain a helium balloon. If you cannot find one, your teacher will have one available in class. Use a standard rubber balloon, not a metallic mylar balloon.
2. Fill a balloon with carbon dioxide. To do so, fill a small soda bottle with vinegar one-quarter full. Roll up a medium handful of baking soda in a paper towel and twist it to fit through the neck of the bottle. Drop the baking soda into the bottle, remove the paper towel, and quickly put the balloon over the mouth. Wait for the balloon to stop inflating and tie it off.

3. Set up a radio or television and stand so that one ear is facing its speaker. Hold the helium balloon 30 cm from the ear facing the sound source and record your observations. Then hold the carbon dioxide balloon 30 cm from the ear and record your observations.

Postlab Questions

1. Helium is less dense than air. Carbon dioxide is more dense than air. When sound travels from air through the CO_2-filled balloon, it gets _____ (focused/spread apart). When sound travels from air through the helium balloon, it gets _____ (focused/spread apart).

2. How would you expect a hydrogen-filled balloon to sound?

3. Does this help explain how it sounds when you're underwater and someone on the surface is yelling to you? Explain why or why not.

This chapter first appeared in Take-Home Physics: 65 High Impact, Low-Cost Labs *(2009), by Michael Horton.*

Chapter 28

Helicopter Seeds and Hypotheses ... That's Funny!

by Leslie Wampler and Christopher Dobson

The most exciting phrase to hear in science, the one that heralds new discoveries, is not "Eureka!" ("I found it!") but "That's funny!"

—Isaac Asimov

Investigating maple samaras, or helicopters seeds, can give students a "that's funny" experience and catalyze the development of inquiry skills. In this article, we describe how to use maple helicopter seeds (samaras) to engage students in focused observation and hypothesis testing. This activity requires only basic classroom equipment and maple samaras, which can be found throughout most of the United States or purchased online.

FLYING FRUIT

Science comes alive for students when it coincides with play. Many students have spent time playing with

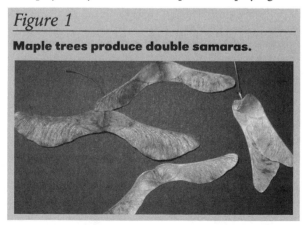

Figure 1

Maple trees produce double samaras.

maple helicopter seeds, also known as whirlybirds. Capture your students' interest by holding up one of these familiar seeds and asking, "Where do these come from? What happens when they fall?" If students are unfamiliar with samaras, give small groups several to observe. Even those who have played with helicopter seeds may be unaware that they contain the seeds of maple trees and are also known as *samaras*. Most, however, will be able to predict that the seeds will twirl or spin as they fall to the ground. At this point, toss the seed into the air and let the class observe its behavior. Build student confidence by celebrating their accurate predictions.

Ask students why they think samaras spin. They may hypothesize that the spinning helps them fly or ride the wind. Have students brainstorm how this motion might benefit maple trees. They should recognize that the helicopter's structure allows for wind-powered seed dispersal. Remind students that plants, like animals, have structures with specialized functions. Fruits are structures that flowering plants produce to disperse their seeds. Some fruits are edible and dispersed by animals. Samaras are dry fruits, specialized for wind dispersal. Maple trees have double samaras (Figure 1), each containing one seed, that usually fall separately.

Now the stage is set for further exploration. Students have drawn on previous knowledge and probably think they know how the samara works. So let's dig deeper.

DOES SIZE REALLY MATTER?

Maple samaras come in a variety of shapes and sizes (Figure 2). It takes more energy to make large samaras. Use guided discussion to encourage students to think about why a plant invests that extra energy and what advantage size gives to a seed. Remind students that seeds contain an embryo (or baby plant) and the food source needed for germination. Large seeds can carry bigger embryos and more nutrients. But what about the wing? Why do maple trees allocate additional energy to the samara's wing? Student responses often relate to the length of time samaras can stay in the air, giving them more opportunity to be carried by the wind.

Does size affect the length of time a samara remains airborne? Let's find out. Hold a "reverse race" between two single samaras of different sizes. The one that stays aloft longer wins. Why would this be an advantage in nature? Hold up the two samara racers. "Ready ... Set ... Wait!" Before dropping the seeds, remind students that science requires focused observation, or thinking about what we see. In math, we ask students to estimate to check their answers; in reading, we ask them to predict what will happen to build reading skills. In science, we ask students to observe carefully, to see with the brain engaged. How can we spot the unusual if we don't know what we expect to see? Scientists are good observers. Science also involves the formation of hypotheses, or possible explanations. Hypotheses are the basis for specific predictions, like whether the large or small samara will stay aloft longer when released simultaneously from the same height. The hypothesis supplies the rationale behind the prediction. Have students provide explanations (hypotheses) for their predictions (Figure 3). Most students predict that the small samara will stay aloft longer because it is lighter, or the big samara will stay in the air longer because of its larger wing. Make sure students understand that predictions allow us to test hypotheses. If the prediction is right, their hypothesis is supported; if not, their hypothesis is falsified.

Finally, we're ready to race. Hold each samara above your head at the same height, gripping the seed with the wing pointing down. Ask a few student volunteers to confirm simultaneous release (controlled variable). Release the seeds and watch as they twirl downward.

TESTING HYPOTHESES

As a class, discuss these questions: Does this outcome confirm our hypothesis? Are there other possible explanations for the result? Is one trial sufficient?

Figure 2

Samaras grow in a variety of shapes and sizes.

PHOTOGRAPHS COURTESY OF THE AUTHORS

Suggest that students investigate for themselves by conducting their own races. Give small groups several large and small samaras for their exploration. Encourage students whose previous predictions were incorrect to show that the result was a one-time fluke and that their hypothesis really is correct. Inform students that wise scientists design experiments with the potential to falsify their hypothesis. If they are unable to falsify it, they tentatively accept the hypothesis, very aware that they may have missed the one experiment that would not support it. This is the tentative nature of science—hypotheses can be strongly supported, but at what point have they been confirmed?

One experiment with the potential to falsify the mass-related hypothesis—small samaras will stay aloft longer because they are lighter—involves separating the seed from the wing in both the small and large samaras. Have students race the two seeds without the wings, sharing their predictions first, as they did with the samara race. If the heavier seed reaches the ground first, the hypothesis is supported. If not, it must be rejected. Use scissors to separate the samaras' wings and seeds. To help students remember which seed and wing came from the larger samara, mark both pieces with a different color dot. Mass the seeds using a balance that can display milligrams. With wings removed, gravity is the primary force influencing downward

Figure 3

Testing your hypothesis

Question: Will a large or small samara stay aloft longer?
Prediction:

Hypothesis (possible explanation for prediction):

Another way to look at this is if your hypothesis is true, then your prediction will occur. Reminder: If your prediction does occur, your hypothesis may still be incorrect—you haven't necessarily proved it!

motion of the seeds. Because acceleration due to gravity is not dependent on mass, the seeds should reach the ground simultaneously if they are released at the same time. Therefore, the mass-related hypothesis is not supported.

If students seem unimpressed, or if some seem to be clinging to the hypothesis that heavier objects fall faster, hold up a sheet of notebook paper and a thick textbook. Ask students which will hit the ground first and why. Crinkle the paper into a ball and drop it at the same time as the book. They will hit the ground at the same time. Clearly, acceleration due to gravity is not dependent on mass.

Because dropping seeds gave a different result than dropping samaras, what would happen if two different-size wings were raced? Students will find that the wing with the larger surface area stays aloft longer, even though it weighs more. Hmmm . . . that's funny! Now your students are ready to use the gray matter between their ears.

WHAT NOW?

At this point, few students will have a hypothesis that fits what we've observed. What will your students suggest the class try next? Encourage questions and suggestions. New discoveries are often the result of curiosity. What else can your students discover about how the parts behave differently from the whole?

We found that small samaras usually stay aloft longer than large ones, although there can be variation in the outcome, depending on release technique. The small samaras that we measured also happened to have lower wing loading (total weight/wing area), a characteristic that results in more lift in aircraft. In plants, rates of descent are correlated with the square root of wing loading for a variety of wind-dispersed species

(Augspurger 1986). The upshot is that neither mass nor wing size alone accounts for the smaller samara's advantage in staying airborne.

Tell students that, when stumped, scientists often return to the observation phase. In other words, it's playtime again! Provide students with rulers and balances, and have them investigate the mass, surface area, and "flight patterns" of intact samaras, as well as their separated constituent parts (seeds and wings). As students apply their freshly honed powers of observation, they will find that samaras spin, wings float down, and seeds merely fall.

Compile class data on the board. Ask for interpretation of the data. Students will see that most of the intact samara's mass is in the seed, while the wing contributes the majority of surface area. The autorotation, or spinning, of the samara results from the combination of the wing's surface area and the off-center concentration of mass in the seed. When samaras fall from a low height without spinning, gravity is the primary force at work and they reach the ground at nearly the same time. See Walker (1981) for a thorough explanation of maple samara aerodynamics.

Ask students for examples of how flowering plants produce fruits to disperse their offspring (seeds) and how different types of fruits are specialized for different types of dispersal (animal, wind, water). In the case of the maple samara, the structure of the fruit (wing) is marvelously designed to accomplish its function of flight. The longer the samara can stay airborne, the greater chance it has of being dispersed from the parent tree by the wind. This is a wonderful example of structure fitting function, one that your students are not likely to forget anytime soon!

EXTENSIONS

Have students manipulate helicopter mass and surface area by applying pieces of tape and clipping the wings, respectively, and then predict the impact on rates of descent (Thomson and Neal 1989).

Connect across the curriculum as highlighted in *Science Scope*'s October 2007 history-of-science issue. Investigate lift and drag using the storyline approach of the Wright brothers and the history of flight (Isabelle 2007). Or use a literature-circle approach, incorporating biographies of the Wright brothers and their invention of flight (Straits 2007).

ACKNOWLEDGMENTS

We would like to acknowledge Dayna Malcolm, Jessica Lilly, and Stephani Johnson for their help with the initial development of this lesson.

References

Augspurger, C. K. 1986. Morphology and dispersal potential of wind-dispersed diaspores of neotropical trees. *American Journal of Botany* 73 (3): 353–363.

Isabelle, A. D. 2007. Teaching science using stories: The storyline approach. *Science Scope* 31 (2): 16–25.

National Research Council (NRC). 1996. *National science education standards*. Washington, DC: National Academies Press.

Straits, W. 2007. A literature-circles approach to understanding science as a human endeavor. *Science Scope* 31 (2): 32–36.

Thomson, J. D., and P. R. Neal. 1989. How-to-do-it wind dispersal of tree seeds and fruit. *The American Biology Teacher* 51 (8): 482–486.

Walker, J. 1981. The amateur scientist: The aerodynamics of the samara: Winged seed of the maple, the ash and other trees. *Scientific American* 245 (4): 226–236.

This article first appeared in the September 2008 issue of Science Scope.

Chapter 29

An Outdoor Learning Center

by the Natural Resources Conservation Services, USDA, and NSTA

LESSON DESCRIPTION

With adults' help, students inventory the school site, develop plans, then create a garden. This raises awareness among students, teachers, and parents about the natural environment and about using the school site for hands-on learning.

Subjects

Art, language arts, mathematics, science, social studies

Time

Prep: 2 hours minimum
Activities: 4 ½–10 hours (not including Extensions)

Further Reading

- "A Garden of Learning: Money Doesn't Have to Be an Obstacle to Valuable Scientific Learning Experiences," from the Summer 2008 issue of *Science and Children*
- "Watching Worms," from *Dig In! Hands-On Soil Investigations* (2001)

TEACHER BACKGROUND

This lesson provides students and teachers with an ongoing opportunity for hands-on environmental education and *resource conservation*.

A readily accessible resource for teaching is the school site. An outdoor learning center (OLC) on the school site offers educators and students an exciting place to observe nature's happenings through the seasons. Right outside the classroom, the school site offers many opportunities to publicize conservation in the neighborhood by improving students' knowledge about and concern for the natural world. By implementing an OLC on the school site, the teacher can maximize teachable moments relating to the environment and *natural resources*.

If your school or neighborhood already has an OLC, skip ahead to the "OLC Activities" section (p. 138).

Enlisting Assistance

Begin the planning process as early as possible. It is important to secure the school administration's permission and obtain support from the school's maintenance staff for your project. If you teach young children, find a teacher of older grades who shares your interest in the project. This teacher's students and yours can become teammates or buddies for the school project. Remember to start small: The project has a greater chance of succeeding if original goals are modest and leave opportunity for growth. As members of the school community see the success of this first step, they may provide support for an OLC for the entire school.

If your school site project has the space and has been well planned, it may be easily adapted for additional outdoor learning activities in continuing school years. If this idea is approved by the administration, you may tell students, parents, and other teachers that this project will be the first step in establishing an OLC on the school site—a place to do hands-on activities, learn about the environment, and participate in actual resource conservation projects. Remember that you are dealing with natural as well as human influences. Be prepared to explain limitations of the OLC, such as temperature, moisture, insects, wind, limited space, or the wrong soil. Learning from this year's activities can help create a more successful OLC next year.

There are many ways to solicit the equipment needed to create and maintain your OLC. Team up with a high-school agricultural program and share supplies. Apply for a grant with a local or national gardening or environmental education association. Ask a landscape firm, local business, or government agency to donate tools.

Creating an OLC Garden

A common and effective school site activity is establishing a garden, which is an environment that students can manipulate. Students' planning, planting, and caring lead to the excitement of harvesting the rewards of their efforts. You can establish a vegetable or flower garden almost anywhere: in a large or small space, on a flat area or on a slope, in the shade or in full sunlight, on the school roof, or on a narrow strip of land between a parking area and the school building. Whichever area is used, the OLC garden provides a venue for short- and long-term environmental learning.

To create a garden, first analyze the site. Students should observe and record the site's physical and environmental characteristics. This class survey provides a starting point and helps show the changes that take place over time. Document modifications to the OLC garden to provide a compete record. After the site has been analyzed, discuss planting, maintaining, and harvesting a garden. The class can then decide on the type of flowers or vegetables to grow, design the garden layout, and plant.

Materials

Actual materials required for this activity depend on the needs identified through the inventory and planning. A soil survey determines the soil type of the school site and helps you select the correct vegetation. Use native plant species whenever possible, since they tend to require less water, weeding, and fertilizer than exotic species. Be sure that none of the plants are invasive, especially if your site is near any natural areas. You can obtain this information from local soil and water conservation agencies.

This activity offers a valuable opportunity to stress safety with your students. Emphasize the correct way to use and treat tools. Ask students to wear pants and shirts with long sleeves on days when they are working outside to avoid insect bites and irritating plants. Teach students what poisonous plants look like and how to avoid such plants. Find out in advance which students have insect and plant allergies, and take necessary precautions.

OLC Activities

The activity, observation, and records of an OLC should be continual and should demonstrate interrelationships between humans and the rest of the natural world. Activities should be inquiry-based and lead to the resolution of issues.

The following suggestions for OLC activities focus on *conservation, beautification*, and wildlife *habitat* improvement:

- Adopt a section of the OLC, a playground, or a nearby stream. Remove all trash and keep the area clean.
- Plant trees or shrubs that shelter the school site from the wind.
- Plant flowers, trees, or grasses to stop soil erosion.
- Invite birds to your area by adding birdhouses near shrubs or trees that provide protection from predators and by choosing plants that provide food and shelter (see Figure 1).
- Create a butterfly garden by using plants and flowers that attract butterflies.
- Order vegetation native to your area and plant a natural landscape.
- Plant grass and trees that are valuable for shade, nesting, and beauty and that vary in color, texture, and shape.
- Adopt a special tree and note seasonal changes, animals that live in the tree, and outstanding characteristics of the tree using photos, drawings, and writing.
- Identify rocks or boulders on the site. Investigate the types of materials used to build the school and compare materials to the rocks on the site.
- Examine a rotting log to observe fungi, moss, and insects.

Figure 1

Plants that provide food for wildlife

Trees	Shrubs	Flowers
Oak	Viburnum	Cosmos
Black Walnut	Blueberry	Impatiens
Crabapple	Dogwood	Marigold
Maple	Lilac	Zinnia
Pine	Sumac	Phlox
Spruce	Pfitzer Juniper	Trumpetvine
Desert Willow	Ocotillo	Desert Baileya
California Buckeye	Desert Huckberry	California Poppy

Some of these plants may not be appropriate for your region. Avoid using nonnative plant species.

- Record temperature, wind, or precipitation over time, and then graph the data.

You might begin by having students classify the environmental events that take place on the school site on a regular and seasonal basis. Students can pass records to succeeding classes to build an environmental history of the site. Over time, students might chart differences in rainfall, snowfall, temperature, growth and death of plants, or erosion. Older students could research the history of the school site. By analyzing history and environmental events through tables, graphs, and written logs, students become more aware of the school site environment.

LEARNING CYCLE

Student Objectives

Students will be able to

- design and build an OLC garden,
- justify the importance of their school-site conservation activities, and
- explain some of the activities or events in the OLC garden.

Materials

For the Class
- Poster board
- Marker
- Local soil survey
- Plastic transparencies
- Overhead markers
- Gardening tools (e.g., hoes, rakes, spades)

- Work gloves
- Plants, trees, and shrubs
- Hose
- Camera (optional)

For Each Student Group
- Diagram of the school site
- Pencil
- Writing paper
- Drawing paper

Perception: 30 minutes–1 hour

1. Introduce students to the idea of an OLC.
2. Begin planning the project by brainstorming ideas for a garden. Let students lead by providing ideas and making notes on the board. What are the students' desires and concerns for the garden? Encourage students to discuss their ideas about planning and placement, and illustrate those ideas on the board and record them.

Exploration: 30 minutes–2 hours

Sketch a simple diagram of the school site.

1. Take the class outside to map the school site. Distribute diagrams of the school site and have students record the physical characteristics of the site. For instance, you might ask students to map areas of bare soil, direct sunlight, vegetation, pavement, and buildings, and compare the slope of the ground in various places. To save time, you can assign each student group to map one characteristic of the site. Then transfer all the maps to clear transparencies and overlay the maps for an overview of the school site.
2. After students have created their maps, suggest to students how they could use this information to create a successful garden. Discuss how students' project ideas would work with the school site's available space. Adjust the plan, as ideas are accepted. This organizing session allows students to communicate, plan, and be responsible for the development of their own school site project.
3. To actively involve older students in the planning process, hold a contest to select the best plans for the garden. Divide students into groups of two or three and ask groups to draw up plans and materials lists of their ideas about what the garden should look like. A panel of teachers, administrators, maintenance staff, and older students choose the top three plans. The class then votes for its favorite plan of the top three.

4. Using the class's suggestions, draw a plan of the garden on poster board.

5. When the project has been finalized, type or print all relevant information and create the formal plan for the school site project.

Application: 3–6 hours

Planning, organizing materials, getting permissions, and involving parents, students, and school staff take several hours. Be sure the adults don't take over the project; this should be a fun and exciting time for student discovery. Also, remember that there is no deadline—this project may never be finished. Ideally, the excitement generated by the school site project will encourage duplicate efforts in the school community and the community at large, starting with home gardens or other beautification activities.

1. Take the class outside and demonstrate the proper use of gardening tools.

2. Split students into small groups or pair students with older teammates or buddies.

3. Assign group roles and responsibilities. Some teams can begin planting while other groups sketch or list more ideas for the garden.

4. Every student should have the opportunity to do some type of gardening activity—raking, planting, etc. Such active participation gives students a sense of ownership for the program and helps them develop a sense of belonging and personal satisfaction.

Evaluation: 30 minutes–1 hour

Evaluation should be an ongoing process as the school site project is developed and includes formal follow-up with students, parents, and other school staff. The students should be allowed to express suggestions for the next phase of the school site project.

Extensions: 30 minutes each, minimum

- Read a story about planting a garden.
- As a class, discuss ideas for expanding the current school site project, develop a plan, and present it to the school administration.
- If an OLC is not possible at your school, identify and label the vegetation currently growing on your school campus. Students can also observe wildlife on your school grounds or in a nearby park.
- Students can grow vegetables or flowers in a garden, using stakes to identify each plant. Choose plants that will produce results before the school year ends.
- If you grow produce in your school garden, try these ideas:

  - Invite a parent to prepare some of the produce grown in the garden.
  - Give produce to the school cafeteria to use in a meal for students.
  - Donate produce to a homeless shelter or soup kitchen.
  - Allow students to divide and take home any produce or flowers.

- Each student can pick a plant in the garden and measure and graph its growth over time. Students can also draw the plant in various stages of growth, or through the seasons.
- Establish a nature trail on or near your school site.
- Take a field trip to a farm or garden center to see how "big" gardens are planted and cared for, or invite a farmer or garden center employee to class to share expertise, experience, and perhaps some plant materials or tools with students.

This chapter first appeared in Dig In! Hands-On Soil Investigations *(2001), from NSTA Press and the Natural Resources Conservation Service, USDA.*

Chapter 30

Inquiry Goes Outdoors

What Can We Learn at the Pond?

by Virginia Bourdeau and Mary E. Arnold

Informal learning environments are ideal settings for students to practice skills necessary for scientific inquiry. Many schools are creating their own school-yard habitats complete with ponds or other water features. A tremendous amount of energy and expense goes into involving students in designing and creating these spaces. Unfortunately, when the habitats are completed, many teachers are unsure how to use them. Traditionally, outdoor education has been equated with *experiential learning*, which may be defined as learning based on personal experiences or direct observation. Experience and observation are key to the scientific inquiry process. Science education can be improved by immersing students in the process of using scientific knowledge to "do" science at their school pond and outdoor learning center.

The Oregon 4-H Wildlife Stewards program has been training teachers and volunteers to convert school grounds to education sites by constructing school-yard wildlife habitats since 1997. In addition, education resources are provided to ensure youth in grades K–8 have rich educational experiences in their habitats. The publication *What Can We Learn at the Pond? 4-H Wildlife Stewards Master Science Leader Guide* (Bourdeau 2004a) (available for $10 at *puborders@oregonstate.edu*) was written to support the program's focus on developing science inquiry skills. Additional information on the 4-H Wildlife Stewards elementary school program

can be found in *Exemplary Science in Grades PreK–4: Standards-Based Success Stories* (Yager and Enger 2006).

LET THE INQUIRY BEGIN! AMAZING AQUATIC PLANTS

Lessons in *What Can We Learn at the Pond? 4-H Wildlife Stewards Master Science Leader Guide* are supported by the Inquiry in Action model, Figure 1 (Bourdeau 2004b, p. 142). This learning model provides a framework for students to use all the steps needed for science as inquiry. Students also have the opportunity to redesign and try again when the results are not as they expected or further questions remain. This supports a student-centered inquiry learning cycle.

Materials

- Two clear plastic jars per team, one additional for a control (0.5 L or similar)
- Algae, collected from the local pond or purchased from a biological supply company
- Elodea (aquatic plant available in aquarium supply stores, two sections, 6 cm long per team (The local aquarium store is often willing to donate this. Cost is less than $5 for a class of 25.)
- Pond water and/or distilled water
- Thermometers

Figure 1

Inquiry in Action model

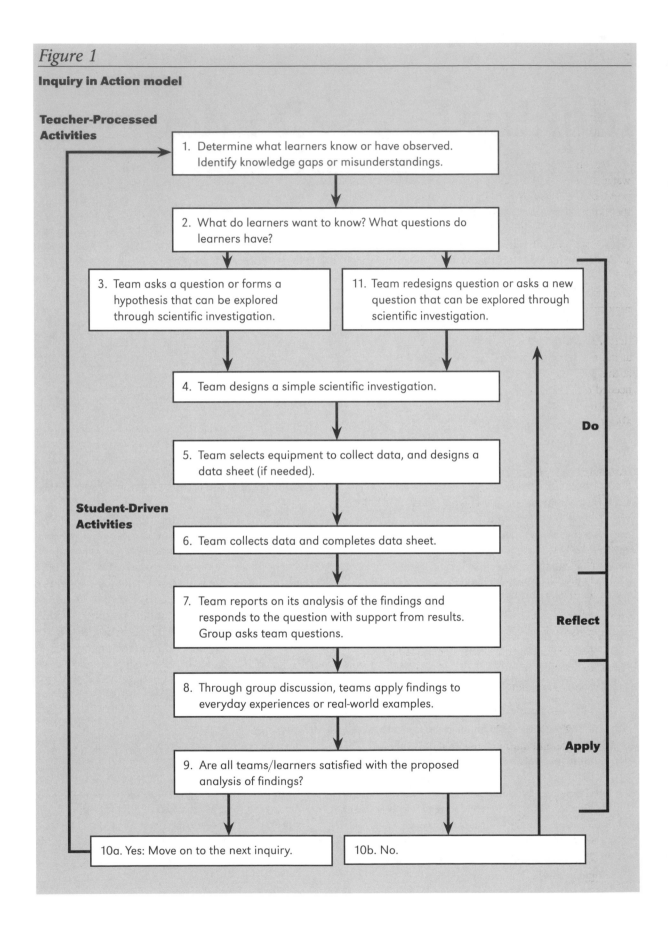

Teacher-Processed Activities

1. Determine what learners know or have observed. Identify knowledge gaps or misunderstandings.

2. What do learners want to know? What questions do learners have?

3. Team asks a question or forms a hypothesis that can be explored through scientific investigation.

11. Team redesigns question or asks a new question that can be explored through scientific investigation.

4. Team designs a simple scientific investigation.

5. Team selects equipment to collect data, and designs a data sheet (if needed).

Student-Driven Activities

6. Team collects data and completes data sheet.

7. Team reports on its analysis of the findings and responds to the question with support from results. Group asks team questions.

8. Through group discussion, teams apply findings to everyday experiences or real-world examples.

9. Are all teams/learners satisfied with the proposed analysis of findings?

10a. Yes: Move on to the next inquiry.

10b. No.

Do

Reflect

Apply

- pH paper
- Variety of "pollutants": salt, vinegar, lemon juice, baking soda, food coloring, soil, home plant fertilizer (dilute for learners' use if needed)
- Various sizes of measuring implements for liquids and solids

As an example, a science class's unit theme is "Can water quality affect the health of plants and algae in the pond community?" We begin by asking students what they know about life in and around ponds (Figure 1, Box 1). This helps determine the skills and understanding students have brought with them. The answers provided by students are recorded on the board. We can now identify any gaps in students' knowledge or misconceptions about ponds. How should these gaps be filled? The teacher may choose to challenge students to do some background research in the library or online if needed. It is also possible that students may discover their own misunderstandings at the end of their experiments. The teacher must decide, at this point in the activity, whether additional research is needed or whether the activity should continue.

Students are asked what they would like to know about the effect of the pollutants in the materials list on plants in the pond community (Figure 1, Box 2). What questions do they have? Student thinking can be guided by asking them questions: Do you know what plants are there? How does water get into the pond? Does the pond level ever get low? Why? Are any of the green organisms in the pond not really plants? Record students' questions on the board. Students' responses will help the teacher identify their areas of interest and plan how the lesson will unfold.

Algae are member of the kingdom Protista. This kingdom contains three groups: the plant-like, animal-like, and fungus-like protists. The plant-like protists include euglenas, diatoms, dinoflagellates, green algae, red algae, and brown algae. A unit on classification could follow this initial lesson to establish students' interest in algae and plants.

Green algae are likely to be found in the school pond or other nearby aquatic environments. Looking at algae under the microscope is a nice addition to this unit because of their many interesting shapes. Prepared slide sets are also available from science suppliers, including interesting samples such as *Spirogyra*, *Chlamydomonas*, and *Volvox*.

Figure 2

Science-Process Skills Inventory

For the following questions, fill in the circle that matches how much you agree with each statement.

		Never	Sometimes	Usually	Always
1.	I can use scientific knowledge to form a question.	O	O	O	O
2.	I can ask a question that can be answered by collecting data.	O	O	O	O
3.	I can design a scientific procedure to answer a question.	O	O	O	O
4.	I can communicate a scientific procedure to others.	O	O	O	O
5.	I can record data accurately.	O	O	O	O
6.	I can use data to create a graph for presentation to others.	O	O	O	O
7.	I can create a display to communicate my data and observations.	O	O	O	O
8.	I can analyze the results of a scientific investigation.	O	O	O	O
9.	I can use science terms to share my results.	O	O	O	O
10.	I can use models to explain my results.	O	O	O	O
11.	I can use the results of my investigation to answer the question I asked.	O	O	O	O

Divide students into several work teams of two to three students each. Each team is asked to choose one of the questions on the board to investigate (Figure 1, Box 3). Teams are encouraged to use an "If . . . , then . . . " hypotheses format for their question. Remind them that they must select only one variable! The question "Does water become warmer in the Sun?" becomes the hypothesis "If we leave water in the Sun, then it becomes too warm to support plant life."

The teacher takes on the role of facilitator and coach, directing the selection of investigative topics and helping each team refine its hypothesis. The teacher helps the groups focus by framing questions using cognitive terminology such as *classify, analyze, predict,* and *create.* Through this interactive process, students are engaged in planning and directing their own learning experiences.

Once each team has created a hypothesis, members of the team design an investigation, determining what information and data they need to collect to test their hypotheses (Figure 1, Boxes 4–5). Each team makes a list of the equipment needed to collect the data and designs a sheet to record the data.

The first time students use the Inquiry in Action model, coaching will be needed at each step. It can be helpful to stop at Box 5 and ask each team to report on their experimental design. In the spirit of encouraging students to do "real science," teachers should allow teams to proceed—even with faulty designs—as long as there are no safety concerns. The inquiry loop provides the opportunity to redesign and continue seeking the right answer (Figure 1, Boxes 10b–11).

Once all the teams have completed their design phase, students are ready to carry out their investigations (Figure 1, Box 6). Will all of the questions selected by the teams be answered on the first try? Probably not. When students begin to use their data to formulate an explanation of their findings, they may generate new questions (Figure 1, Box 7). Teams can collaborate and share data. For instance, one team may realize it should have taken the water temperature at the pond, but another team has done so, and they can share their results.

With the assistance of the teacher, students can conduct library research or design further investigations at the pond or in the laboratory to continue their learning. Provide an open environment for the teams of students to continue to ask their own questions and direct their own learning. Students may wish to create models to test new explanations.

To complete the scientific inquiry process, learners communicate their results through written reports, posters, displays, or presentations. These may happen in class or be the basis of a science fair or family science night.

ASSESSMENT

The Science-Process Skills Inventory (Arnold and Bourdeau 2007) (Figure 2, p. 143) is used as a pretest/post-test evaluation instrument for the skills students practiced in this lesson. The Science-Process Skills Inventory was developed to measure the overall ability of students to understand and use the range of skills related to the cycle of science inquiry. These skills include forming scientific questions, designing scientific procedures, collecting and recording data, analyzing results, using models to describe results, and creating scientific presentations. These are the skills students practice as they use the Inquiry in Action model. The Science Process Skills Inventory contains 11 items. Respondents are asked to rate each statement using a four-point Likert scale, indicating their level of use of the science skill associated with each statement: (1) never, (2) sometimes, (3) usually, and (4) always.

CONCLUSION

The school pond can provide the context for real-world application of science as inquiry at any grade level. It is up to the teacher to present learning themes in a way that allows learners to practice the abilities necessary to do scientific inquiry and become more scientifically literate. To accomplish this goal, the learning that begins at the pond should also be taken to the next step. Remember to ask students, "How does what we learn at this pond apply to your world beyond school?"

References
Arnold, M. E., and V. Bourdeau. 2007. The Science Process Skills inventory. *http://oregon.4h.oregonstate.edu.*
Bourdeau, V. 2004a. *What can we learn at the pond? 4-H wildlife stewards master science leader guide* (4-H 3101L). Corvallis, OR: Oregon State University Extension and Experiment Station Communications.
Bourdeau, V. 2004b. 4-H experiential education—A model for 4-H science as inquiry. *Journal of Extension* 42 (5). *www.joe.org/joe/2004october/tt3.shtml.*
Yager, R. E., and S. K. Enger, eds. 2006. *Exemplary science in grades PreK–4: Standards-based success stories.* Arlington, VA: National Science Teachers Association.

This article first appeared in the September 2008 issue of Science Scope.

Chapter 31
Schoolyard Geology

by Beverly Hagberg and Donna R. Sterling

"Can we break rocks again today?" This question is typical of the excitement students show for identifying rock types after they apply their rock identification knowledge to the geology in the schoolyard. Many schoolyards, although bulldozed during construction, still exhibit telling outcrops of the underlying bedrock. Armed with a few materials, you can discover what is just outside your door while modeling the joy of doing science. This activity fits into the curriculum after the rock cycle and igneous, sedimentary, and metamorphic rock identification labs.

SCHOOLYARD FIELD TRIP PLANNING

Start by taking a walk around the school property and local vicinity yourself. Determine the school boundaries if they are not obvious, so that you do not wander off campus. While on your personal field trip, check rock types often and decide whether each rock type is part of the local rock group or something brought in during school construction. Take a school map to mark where actual rock outcrops of bedrock exist. Identify rocks and take collected samples to knowledgeable colleagues to see if they agree.

If a great outcrop is nearby and within easy walking distance, set up a field trip to take students off school property. Be sure to scout and address any safety issues that may exist beforehand. Geologists, park rangers from local parks, or local university geology departments are often willing to come to assist you. This is also a good time to involve parents as chaperones, particularly if you have large classes or will be taking all of your students in one large group.

Before heading out on the field trip, remind students to wear old tennis shoes and full-length jeans. Make and review with students a safety plan for crossing streets, climbing stream banks, and walking through busy parking lots and on uneven terrain. Encourage them to wear rubber-soled shoes. Ahead of time, determine if there are areas to be totally avoided. If there is any danger from falling rocks, you must obtain hard hats for all participants. Safety glasses are needed for using rock hammers and chemical-splash goggles for using vinegar.

In the classroom, practice using a rock hammer and materials to identify rock types. Review how

Further Reading

*   "Sand: Up Close and Amazing," from the September 2003 issue of *Science Scope*

vinegar produces carbon dioxide bubbles when rock contains carbonates. Students can also learn to use a Brunton compass to find the *strike* (rock-bed direction) and *dip* (tilt). Share with students that David Brunton, a Canadian surveyor who worked in Colorado, developed a small compass because he became tired of carrying heavy equipment while surveying. In 1894, he patented his compass, which was made by a local watchmaker (see Internet Resources).

Strike and dip are difficult concepts to teach. Using the analogy of a simple roof often helps students understand. First, students need to understand a fold in strata, which is shown in most textbooks and can be illustrated by bending a peanut butter and jelly sandwich to show folding of layers. Then compare the direction of a ridge to the direction of the folded sandwich to a rooftop. The roof needs to be straight with no fancy L- or T-shaped rooflines. Strike is the direction of the top of the roofline and dip is the angle of the roof. Scientists can measure the direction (strike) of an outcrop and the angle of its tilt (dip), much like a roof (see Internet Resources for an online graphic).

DAY OF FIELD TRIP

Prepare a relevant section of a local topographic map, clearly mark the points of interest for the field trip and dangerous areas, and distribute it to students as the itinerary for field trip day. On the day of your schoolyard exploration, each team should pick up rock-identification equipment, maps, and books, and quickly check to make sure everything is there before leaving the classroom (see Figure 2 for a materials list). Groups of two or three students transport their own sets of materials. Before allowing students to do any hammering, model the proper technique. First, put on your goggles and gloves. Next, explain how the weathering of the rock determines which side of the hammer they should use. Finally, shout "Heads up!" or "Hammer!" to warn everyone to back away from the strike zone. You may also want to take a few improper swings at the rock and ask students to explain what was unsafe with your technique.

On your walk, as students find and identify rock samples, ask them to determine if the rock is local or was brought in during construction. (It is local if found in an outcrop of bedrock. Small, loose samples cannot be considered local.) Only test a sample with vinegar if you believe the sample is limestone or dolomite. Chemical-splash goggles and gloves are required during testing. Be careful to set the presumed limestone or dolomite on steady ground and leave it untouched after testing. The less students handle the vinegar, the better. Use the field guide to identify the name of the rock sample. Ask students to label a plastic bag with the correct name and place the rock sample in it. Their labels should include the location and date where the rock was found. Once you return to the classroom, place your finds in a central location with their labels. For homework, students bring in a rock from their backyard that they believe is part of the bedrock.

DAY AFTER THE FIELD TRIP

Start a discussion by asking questions such as, "If this is igneous [sedimentary, metamorphic, etc.], how did it get here?" This discussion can take many twists and turns. Confirm plausible explanations. Have students place the rocks they brought in as homework on a table everyone can gather around, and place rocks from their field trip on a separate part of the table. The homework rocks can be identified and compared to

Figure 1

A metamorphic rock outcrop

PHOTO COURTESY OF THE AUTHORS

Figure 2

Materials
- Rock hammer
- Field guide to rocks
- Geologic map of local area, see *www.Usgs.Gov*
- Small, plastic, capped bottle of vinegar
- Paper towels
- Brunton compass
- Resealable plastic bags for samples
- Local topographic map as a field trip map
- Safety goggles
- Chemical-splash goggles
- Gloves
- Labels

those found on school grounds and the geologic map of the local area. Ask students which rocks appear to be part of the bedrock and why. Then have students place all rocks that do not appear to be part of the bedrock together and think about what might be the history behind these. Some may be identified as remnants of construction or landscaping, and others may be from an intrusive layer or even rock brought back from a vacation. Identify what you see using a combination of your resources.

FIELD TRIP EXTENSION AND ASSESSMENT

Extend learning by having students choose one of the following activities, which they will share with the class. This can be done individually or in small groups and usually takes two or three days of classwork and homework.

- Research and write the story of a local rock formation.
- Build a container for classified and labeled rocks.
- Construct a timeline delineating the life and changes of the local geology.
- Draw or create a computer-generated series of pictures depicting the changes in local geology that happened in the past to result in the present landscape.
- Compose lyrics to describe the geologic evolution of local geology.
- Interview a local geologist to find more details than those discussed in class.

If there are no outcrops on your school property or nearby, there are still ways to teach local geology. Make students aware of outcrops and road cuts in the local vicinity where they can see bedrock. They are easily found in hills blasted out during construction or in eroded stream banks. Another idea is to use books such as the *Roadside Geology* for your state (see Internet Resources). The teacher can make some of the nearby road trips, take pictures, and collect samples to share with the students. Internet searches of the geology of your state often result in university sites with useful information, which could be used to write a webquest of local geology.

This schoolyard field trip can be an inexpensive, but rich, learning experience for middle school students. It places rock samples in their hands while putting the nature of science in their heads. With planning on the teacher's part, this flexible, community-based field trip can be used year after year.

Internet Resources

Patent for Brunton Pocket Transit
http://americanhistory.si.edu/collections/surveying/object.cfm?recordnumber=761553

Strike and Dip
http://geog.unt.edu/~williams/images/strike.htm

Roadside Geology
http://geology.com/store/roadside-geology.shtml

This article first appeared in the December 2008 issue of Science Scope.

PART

5

Funds and Materials

Chapter 32

You *Can* Get What You Want

Tried-and-True Tips for Securing Funds and Resources From the Community

by Yvonne Delgado

Many teachers regularly use their own money during the year to pay for miscellaneous teaching materials or to help individual students in need. What if I told you that you could secure all the funds and resources for anything that you want to do educationally for your classroom? It's no fantasy; it's simply a matter of thinking ahead and expending some up-front energy for some great returns on the time investment.

COMMON MATERIALS

Let's first talk about securing common materials or supplies. Let's say you need clear plastic pop bottles to fill with water to make Cartesian divers for science. Possibly you're even getting sick of drinking all that pop, rinsing bottles, and carrying them to school. What if you could get all the clear plastic water bottles you needed—clean bottles, bottles with lids, and bottles already full of water. This would be an easy task. Look in the phone book. Find some water companies or grocery stores in the local vicinity. If you need just a few bottles, you can ask any local company. The more you need, the more you may want to approach a larger organization, and the more closely you would want to match your request with their product line. Call first; let them know you're looking for water

bottle donations. Find out the name of the person who handles such requests. Know exactly what you want (specific size, quantity, shape, color) before calling, and then ask for it. I shoot for the ideal, and most of the time I get what I ask for.

Be prepared with the following information:
- Your name, title, and connection to the project
- Name of school, location, contact information
- Number of classrooms and students being served
- In some instances, demographics are also helpful (e.g., percentage of students not graduating, number of minority students, number of students who receive free and reduced lunch, number of students by gender)
- Subject area
- General age range of students
- Exact item specifications and quantity needed
- Date items are needed (give yourself some leeway; don't cut it too close)
- What is in it for the company or organization (e.g., good public relations)

Steps in securing donations:
- List needs and wants prior to the start of the school year or the project start date.
- Gather all information.

- Be specific on exactly what you want (e.g., five 3' × 5' pieces of sod).
- Try to match requests with company product lines.
- Be prompt picking up items.
- Send a timely thank-you (whenever appropriate, I promote their donation in flyers, news releases, or publications).

Some examples of commonly requested items are batteries, spools of wire, fabric, special types of paper, pens or markers, paper cups—the list is endless. As for quantity, ask for what you need. If you need only a couple items because you are demonstrating something, then ask only for that. If you need enough for a group of students, ask for enough for each student plus a couple extra. The companies will do their best to meet your request or assist as much as they can. Once I needed candy for a mathematics sorting project. I wrote a letter explaining the information as outlined on this page and requested five bags of a specific type of candy. I stopped in, talked to the manager, explained my request, and handed him my letter. The next day he called and donated a $25 gift card from the store, which more than satisfied my candy purchase.

PROFESSIONAL VOLUNTEERS

Another type of need is to find people to construct larger or more complex project components. Again, use your local resources and collect community information. As you drive around your community, collect the names of the local companies you pass on the way. When you talk to parents, make note of what organizations they work for. Read the local papers; find out who's who in the business community. These are the types of long-term relationships that you want to cultivate. Keep the company names, individual contacts, and phone numbers in your computer, PDA, or phone.

When I embark on an environmental project, for example, I call in volunteers from the local parks, the county soil and water department, and environmental agencies. I also contact specialists from local businesses and other subject matter experts. If I'm working on an autism project, I contact school special education staff, local autism nonprofits, parents with autistic children, and so on. It has been my experience that most everyone is willing and able to assist if given enough notice. I would recommend at least one month of lead time to secure a volunteer.

Working with a team allows the responsibilities to be split into reasonable workloads. Recently I worked on a project to update and enhance our existing erosion lesson. I called and secured a volunteer from each of the following organizations—the local park system, the county soil and water department, and one other local science education specialist. I then set a series of team meetings—one hour every two weeks for a period of three months. We selected the meeting time to best meet the needs of the team players. Two teachers were the team leaders and met with the team every two weeks. At the first meeting, we provided the team with a general overview and project expectations—complete with a timeline and any budgetary information. These local subject matter experts took our teachers out to sites to see real examples of erosion. In addition, they were able to share valuable information about the various types of erosion, what additional problems arise with erosion, and contemporary erosion control practices. The volunteers assisted with building some of the erosion demonstration models, donated literature and other materials for the classroom, gave examples of how they teach the topic to students, and overall provided our teachers with a great educational experience that could be shared with the students.

Another option to consider is contacting local colleges, vocational schools, or trade schools. Often teachers in these institutions are looking for opportunities

Examples of Donations

Here is a sampling of the donations of resources and time I have secured over the years:

- College professors providing professional development for our teaching staff
- Lunches from local restaurants for a summer educational program
- Donations for a basket to be auctioned off at a charitable event
- Dry ice for science experiments
- Labor for installing new carpeting and painting classrooms
- Computers for teaching staff
- Laptop and projector for teaching
- Three years of maintenance of our microscopes
- Paper, markers, paints, cardboard, cups, etc., for various science events
- Baking soda, vinegar, candies, sugar, salt, etc., for various science experiments
- Local scientists, artists, actors, and authors to provide authenticity to a subject (either as a guest speaker, to assist with a project, or to demonstrate their craft)
- Time to judge a science event
- Gift certificates as special prizes for students
- Books on a specific subject for students

to engage their students in real projects. For example, after receiving funds from a grant to purchase wiring, I asked electrical students from a vocational school to come in and rewire our program's computers. It was a win-win situation for all involved.

Points to consider when asking for volunteers:
- Gather your information.
- Be specific about the project needs and parameters.
- Be sure to let them know what their commitment involves: number of meetings, approximate amount of time at each meeting, deadline for the project.
- Let them know from where the funds are coming for the materials and supplies.
- Be sensitive to their time needs—keep meetings on schedule and limit meetings to only what is needed.
- Always remember to send a thank-you note upon project completion or once you have received your items. I sometimes include a photograph or have students sign the thank-you note. Often, these professionals are flattered that you recognized them and their ability to contribute to an important educational project.

MORE COMPLEX PROJECTS

Donations have enhanced our science program in many ways, but two of my favorite examples demonstrate how such contributions can make a huge difference in your science curriculum.

Connecting to the Standards

This article relates to the following *National Science Education Standards* (NRC 1996).

Teaching Standards
Standard F:
Teachers of science actively participate in the ongoing planning and development of the school science program.

Program Standards
Standard D:
The K–12 science program must give students access to appropriate and sufficient resources, including quality teachers, time, materials and equipment, adequate and safe space, and the community.

When our science department decided to build erosion tables to use for hands-on Earth science investigations of erosion, we needed sod and sand. So I identified companies who specialized in each of these areas—a nursery and a sand company. Our tables have three columns each—one holds sod and two hold sand. As we gathered information for the nursery, we had to measure each column to determine the exact dimensions. With the dimensions in hand, we approached the nursery and were provided with a bundle of sod that we cut to fit the columns. The cutting was more difficult than we anticipated, so the following year we asked nursery staff to assist us with cutting the sod into the proper dimensions. For the sand donation, we needed to specify the grade and quantity. We first had to experiment to get the proper grade that would best demonstrate erosion, which we did. The volunteers so enjoyed working on creating these indoor environmental learning activities, we are now working together to design an outdoor component.

Another special feature of our science classroom made possible through donations are two 180 gal. aquariums provided to us through a grant from the Hershey Foundation. One aquarium houses native Ohio pond fish and animals. The other is home to native Ohio stream fish and animals. The stream tank also has a chiller and flow system to best simulate the natural environment of a stream. We use these tanks to teach classification, habitat, and the water cycle. To help offset the costs of maintaining the tanks, local bait shops were approached for donations of feed—which they gladly gave. We continue to value each and every contribution to our many projects.

Although it can seem impossible to accomplish some of the projects we dream of doing with our students, with a little help, you can do a lot. So the next time a blockbuster idea for a new learning project strikes, instead of feeling limited by a lack of dollars or supplies, grab a list of Who's Who from the local Chamber of Commerce. Remember, you'll never know unless you ask!

Reference
National Research Council (NRC). 1996. *National science education standards*. Washington, DC: National Academies Press.

This article first appeared in the Summer 2008 issue of Science and Children.

Chapter 33

Need Money? Get a Grant!

Tips on Writing Grants for Classroom Materials and Larger Items

By Linda Bryson

They say necessity is the mother of invention. I guess that's how I became my school's resident grant writer. It's not that I had particular gifts as a writer or an uncanny sense of persuasion or even a special gift of gab. What I had was a need, and the need was for money! The first grant I received was a Lysol/NSTA award in 2001. That grant gave me $1,000 to spend on registration, travel, and housing so I could attend NSTA's National Conference in San Diego, California, as well as $500 to purchase classroom supplies. It wasn't a lot of money, but it did inspire me to try my hand at applying for additional grants. Once I got started, I couldn't stop. After I obtained countless grants and brought more than $20,000 in money and materials to my school as a result of these efforts, people started asking *me* for help getting grants. So I've pulled together a few of my favorite tips to help you get started finding that most elusive of resource— money—for your classroom. If I could only figure out how to get some more time. . . .

WORK THE INTERNET

The internet is one of the easiest ways to locate potential grants. Typing in a general search for "teacher grant money" gets you started. Different search engines give different results. For example, Google results differ from Yahoo! results, which differ from those found on Mamma.com (I usually have good luck with Mamma). This may seem strange, but I sometimes get different results for the same search at different times during the day, so be sure to try different times as well.

As soon as I get the search results, I e-mail them to myself. Believe me, it's easier to delete an e-mail link that you are no longer interested in than to feel like kicking yourself for not being able to find the link again.

I start by eliminating the grants I don't qualify for by looking at grade level and state requirements under "eligibility requirements." A grant may sound great, but it may not be appropriate for you, so don't waste any of your valuable time.

If you do qualify by grade level and state, then give every grant a chance. The title of a grant could make you think that it isn't for you, but if you look closely, there may be something there. For example, I learned of the Lysol/NSTA grant from an e-mail from NSTA that contained information about the elementary grant. The title Lysol/NSTA didn't initially spark any connections to my curriculum. However, I read the grant application carefully and found that it was something that interested me. While the majority of the winners had projects about sneezing, blowing their noses, and germs, my winning project was on monarch butterflies. I had read the grant application's fine print, which said the proposal could be on any topic. And my project was something that I had completed previously with my students, which made it easy for me to write it up at a busy time of the year—another useful tip to file away when considering applying for grants.

GATHER SCHOOL DATA

Once you decide to apply for a grant for which you are qualified, carefully read the fine print to make sure you meet all of the requirements. For this part, you will probably also need to know some basic information about your school, such as the population breakdown by ethnicity or maybe the percentage of students who receive free lunches. This information is available through your state's department of education. Unfortunately, this information may be more than a year old. Your current school's population breakdown is available through your district's central office, and you may have to ask around to find someone who knows the current data. Fortunately, computers have made this information available at a person's fingertips.

STORE YOUR STUFF

Once you have some basic information, you may need it for another grant application, so store it in a special folder or notebook. I use a pocket folder with brad fasteners. Any grant-related information that I need to keep for future reference gets holes punched into it and fastened into the middle section of the folder. Any completed grant applications also get added to the middle section. I use the folder's pockets for other grant-related items—one pocket for grants that I might be considering and the other for incomplete applications.

If you print out a grant application with several pages, make sure to staple it together before you insert it into a pocket. It is easier to have the pages all together when you are looking for it again at a later time. As time goes by, periodically clean out your grants folder to keep it up-to-date.

GIVE THE DATE ITS DUE

A proposal's due date is probably the most important piece of information in the application process. It may be a busy time of the year, so you have to realistically decide if it is something that you are going to be able to complete before the due date. I submitted one grant application in a 48-hour period of time, and I could do it because I had all of my information already

organized. Still, I was shocked when I found out that I had won the grant, because I had completed the actual write-up in less than two hours.

COMPLETE THE APPLICATION

Once you begin filling out your grant application, make sure to complete all sections. Read and then reread the questions to make sure you understand what information is required. Some grants have links to frequently asked questions where the organization has already taken the time to give a more thorough explanation to some basic questions.

If you can, work with a peer or friendly critic, then have him or her read over the application to make sure that your answers are clear and appropriate.

If there is a section marked "optional," complete that, too. Even if it says optional, I don't take any chances and supply the information.

For some grants, you must send a letter of intent before receiving the actual grant application. If this is a requirement, write up your letter, show it to your administrator, and then ask if it can be copied onto

---

Figure 1

A selection of helpful grant resources

Grant Resources From NSTA
Grants, Grants, Grants
http://sciguides.nsta.org/internet/grants.aspx
NSTA's Webwatchers program has compiled a list of online resources to help you find grant money and to help you get it.

NSTA Teacher Awards and Competitions
www.nsta.org/awardscomp
A listing of other awards and opportunities available through NSTA

Other Grant Opportunities
Best Buy Teach Awards
http://communications.bestbuy.com/communityrelations/teach.asp

Target Field Trip Grants
http://sites.target.com/site/en/corporate/page.jsp?contentId=PRD03-002537

Verizon Foundation
http://foundation.verizon.com
Click on "apply for grants" to learn more.

---

your school's letterhead. The school letterhead gives more credence to your request.

If the application is sent via the internet, sometimes it is a good idea to print out the application first to view the overall grant requirements in one place. This will also allow you a chance to gather any necessary information before you actually sit down and begin filling out the application. Use your folder or notebook and have all of the needed information at your fingertips, so you don't have to start and stop or get up because you need to find another piece of information. I also find that using a highlighter to mark important information is helpful. Printing out the confirmation sheet that you receive after you send the application provides a reminder for later.

LOOK IN MANY PLACES

There is no one single place for grants—grants are everywhere, even places you might not think. Grants for specialized areas of interest are also often sent through e-mails. Join an organization, and get on their e-mail lists. As a member of NSTA and NSTA's Building a Presence, I receive e-mails about numerous opportunities. Even if it is not appropriate for me or my school, it only takes a minute to forward an e-mail to someone who may find the opportunity of interest. That road goes two ways—if you pass along opportunities that may interest others and let the word out that you are interested in applying for grant money, they in turn may be likely to pass along opportunities they come across that are appropriate for you.

Many national grants may come from unexpected places. For example, national retailers, such as Best Buy,

Connecting to the Standards

This article relates to the following *National Science Education Standards* (NRC 1996):

Teaching Standards
Standard D:
Teachers of science design and manage learning environments that provide students with the time, space, and resources needed for learning science.

Verizon, and Target may have educational grants on their websites. Check them out. (See Figure 1 for more grant ideas.)

SPREAD THE WEALTH

I have written many grants in the same school year for similar materials. This past year, I wrote several grants for computer projection equipment. I started off by having just my name on the first grant application. As the school year went by, I asked other staff members if I could include their names on the grant. That way, if I receive a grant, other teachers in my building will benefit if I get another one. I give duplicate materials to someone else in our building. So far, all of my colleagues have been happy to be added to the grant applications.

Working with other supportive technology staff members, if you need some guidance, is also helpful. On one grant for classroom computer equipment, I included the librarian's name in the grant, but by working with our district's technology staff, we ended up equipping my classroom *and* the library. That made a lot of us happy.

I also tear out clippings about grants from professional newspapers and magazines. They go into the folder's pocket until I have the time to read them over.

BRACE FOR SUCCESS!

Once people in your area see that you are successful at grant writing, they will want to talk to you. I have worked with middle and high school teachers in our area on grant writing. I give a short introduction to get them started and then turn them loose in a computer lab. They work for hours and say very little because everyone is interested in finding money to spend in their classrooms! With a little perseverance, they'll find it!

Resource
National Research Council (NRC). 1996. *National science education standards.* Washington, DC: National Academies Press.

This article first appeared in the Summer 2007 issue of Science and Children.

Chapter 34

Science on a Shoestring

Stock Your Shelves With Free and Inexpensive Science Materials

by Sandy Watson

M ost of us have experienced the frustration of limited school science budgets, and many of us have had to resort to repeatedly dipping into our personal funds to finance the material needs of our classrooms. Certainly there are some items, such as chemicals and safety equipment, that must be ordered from educational science supply companies, but there are many other items that can be acquired at little or no cost to the teacher or school system. With a little time and effort, you can start the school year with adequately stocked science supply shelves.

Before beginning your search for materials, check to see if your school has a policy governing the use of items that have been donated or obtained from nontraditional sources (such as local businesses). Also, double-check your budget for the year and review your school's reimbursement policy before spending any of your own money. Also, take a look through the laboratory activities you have done in the past and want to repeat, and create a list of materials for each activity. If you are looking for low-cost labs to substitute for more expensive activities, Figure 1, page 160, lists websites where labs that use inexpensive materials can be found. Peruse those sites and see if anything appeals to you. Save the labs that you feel you could duplicate and add the necessary materials to your supply list. Figure 2 on page 160 is a sample list of inexpensive

and free science supplies that you can send home to parents with a request for donations. This list can also be posted in the teachers' lounge.

Great places to begin your search for classroom supplies are yard sales, garage sales, and flea markets. Be sure to take your list with you and be prepared to dig through boxes. Some people will place a box of toys out and it will be up to you to search through it for balls, marbles, small cars, and other items on your list. Once they learn you are a teacher and are looking for items to use with your students, many people will discount the price of some items or even donate them. I once obtained a large box of more than 150 brand-new amber dropper bottles at no cost from a yard sale when I mentioned I was a teacher and planned to use them in class.

Everyday items often found at yard sales can also be used in the science lab. If you have the need for a class set of mortars and pestles, but find them too expensive, search for metal spoons at yard sales. The back of a metal spoon works very well as a grinding tool (use a piece of wax paper to grind on). Hot plates are also often found at garage sales. I have six that I use and all were purchased at yard sales (none for more than a couple of dollars). Consider picking up plastic storage containers for storing your materials. I have found that square plastic food containers are great for holding small items such as marbles, balloons, and toy cars. Many larger storage bins with lids and handles can be found at these sales at bargain prices. Yard sales are unpredictable; you never know what you might discover. My prize find was a digital scale in great working condition that cost me only a dollar.

Other resources for science materials include local businesses such as hardware stores, film developing centers, newspaper offices, large corporations, medical clinics, doctors' offices, and bait shops. It is always a good idea to bring your school identification card or a letter from your school principal on school letterhead. My local hardware store offers discounts to teachers and free services. For example, when I needed a set of ramps, I asked my local hardware store to cut a set of eight 3 ft. long sections of 1 in. × 6 in. pine. They also routed out a groove in the center of each plank (for a marble to roll along) at no charge. We only had to pay the cost of the wood itself and that was at a discount. The entire set of eight ramps ended up costing less than $25. That is quite a savings over the $95 per ramp listed in my science supply catalog. In such cases, a thank-you card is also suggested.

There are numerous uses for film canisters in the science classroom. These can be obtained free of charge from most film development centers. One of these centers was located in a local grocery store. I asked them to start saving the canisters for me and they were more than happy to do so. Once a month, I stop by and pick up a large box filled with canisters that I share with the entire science department. A local newspaper office donates the blank end-rolls of newsprint to area teachers. These end-rolls are available in various widths and are great to use for many types of activities.

Many physicians are willing to donate anatomical and physiological posters and models and old medical journals to science teachers. Medical clinics are another resource for science materials. I obtained a set of old x-rays (with patients' identifying information removed) from one clinic that I used when I taught the human skeletal system. My classroom windows worked as great light boxes when I taped the x-rays directly to them.

Figure 1

Science lesson plan websites

Discovery Education—
http://school.discovery.com/lessonplans/physci.html

Life Science and Biology Lesson Plans—
www.accessexcellence.org/AE/AEC/AEF

Educator's Reference Desk—
www.eduref.org/cgi-bin/lessons.cgi/Science

GoENC—
www.goenc.com

Academy Curricular Exchange—
http://ofcn.org/cyber.serv/academy/ace/sci/high.html

Science Lesson Plans and Resources—
www.cloudnet.com/~edrbsass/edsci.htm

Teachers First Lesson Plans—
www.teachersfirst.com/matrix.htm

LessonPlansPage—
www.lessonplanspage.com/ScienceJH.htm

Figure 2

Free and inexpensive science materials list

- Small cars (velocity)
- Marbles (velocity)
- Balloons (to show air has mass or capture yeast gas production)
- Metal spoons (mortars)
- Plastic containers (storage)
- Hot plates (heat)
- Pots (heat water)
- Aluminum pie pans (various uses)
- Magnifying glasses
- Balls (gravity and energy transfer)

- Heavy items such as fishing weights, large bolts, etc. (density)
- Tubs to hold water (density)
- Aquarium supplies
- Dropper bottles (pH experiments and biological stains)
- Craft supplies (for creative projects)
- Colored pencils, crayons, and markers (drawing activities)
- Rulers, compasses (rulers can be used as marble ramps)
- Magnets

- Simple machines (screwdrivers and tweezers)
- Flashlights (light and color)
- Baby-food jars and other small containers (volume)
- Science books
- Clay (to hold burning candles to observe chemical change)
- Candles (birthday and larger)
- Measuring cups and spoons
- Disposable cups and plates
- String
- Playing cards (probability lessons)
- Pot holders

I found another source of materials in a local pulpwood mill that housed a chemical laboratory. They periodically donate a large supply of chemical laboratory glassware such as distillation tubes, specimen bottles, graduated cylinders, test tubes, and beakers. Of course, donated glassware must be thoroughly cleaned, sterilized, and inspected for cracks and chips before use by students.

I also frequently drop by the local bait shop to pick up night crawlers, crickets, and minnows to use in my biology classes. The local butcher is a great source for free animal organs, such as pig hearts, lungs, kidneys, and eyes, for in-class dissections.

One of the laboratory investigations that I use requires friction blocks, rectangular sections of wood with sandpaper attached to one side and an eyehook at one end. They cost $5–10 each when purchased from a science education supply catalog. Instead of buying friction blocks, I made my own set. I noticed that workers at a local construction site had amassed a large pile of wood blocks of various sizes and were preparing to burn them when I stopped by and asked if I could have some. I sanded down the rough edges, purchased a set of eyehooks, and screwed one into an end of each block. Instead of gluing sandpaper to the blocks, I have students drag the blocks across sheets of sandpaper set on top of the lab table (one student will have to hold the sandpaper in place or it can be secured with masking tape).

Online auction houses such as eBay are another source of potentially cheap science materials. I recently purchased a dozen brand-new spring scales for $5. These scales sell for more than $6 each in science supply catalogs. I have also purchased microscope slides and coverslips, a model of a frog, and other items at steeply discounted prices from these online auction sites. At my school, we found it much cheaper to buy common household items used in laboratories (such as sodium chloride, ammonia, baking soda, cornstarch, and vinegar) in bulk from local discount warehouses rather than pay the prices charged by commercial supply houses.

Teaching science can be costly but it doesn't always have to be. Start your collection adventure now and you could soon be running out of storage space.

This article first appeared in the February 2007 issue of Science Scope.

Chapter 35

Got Stuff?

by Antonio M. Niro

When I began teaching many years ago, I was given a textbook that I estimate went into print sometime shortly after Gutenberg put monks out of business and just before *Sputnik* flew. Recently, a newly completed high school created the need for a new middle school, which in turn forced a new crisis—lots of students and no money for science supplies.

I learned quickly that science teachers have to be creative with limited funds to generate the equipment they need to accomplish hands-on science lab activities. Essentially, I had to "get stuff." Funds were lean during those times, but I needed ways and materials to teach heat, light, sound, magnetism, electricity, work, energy, and simple machines. I found great ideas for experiments from science books, sports, hobby magazines, journals, colleagues, conferences, the internet, and educational TV programs; however, I still needed the equipment to conduct hands-on activities.

So how do I get the stuff? To start, I asked students to bring in items; I went to local businesses; I pressed family and friends, but I did not generate enough, or the right kind of, materials. After brainstorming and rethinking my plan of attack, I decided to try a scavenger hunt. Students were given a list of materials to gather. I had created the list first from a textbook equipment list and then added to it based on a plan to conduct specific activities and experiments. Other items were added to the list while planning the materials that would be needed for future student demonstrations.

Because we were starting from scratch and generating materials for six teachers, my list was long—nearly 200 items. For your needs, consider including items that are consumables so budgeted school funds can be used to purchase permanent or expensive equipment that serve the whole school. Your list will vary based on the needs of your staff. In addition to the list, a letter was distributed for each student to take home a week before the deadline (see Figure 1, p. 164).

At a meeting of the parent-teacher organization, I explained what I had in mind and asked for their help, particularly with publicity and logistics. They got the word out through school notices, as well as the local newspaper and radio. In addition, they pledged a small financial commitment of about $50 to fund a pizza party for the winners. The approval of the administration was secured once the plan was finalized.

The rules of the hunt were simple: Students were given about one week to gather items; any amount of time longer than that fosters the "I've got plenty of time" attitude and may result in diminished returns. Point values were given to items depending on their rarity, availability, or desirability. Disposable items such as aluminum foil or string were assigned five points. More desirable items such as tools or games were valued at 10 points. Permanent things such as an oscilloscope or a record player earned the greatest points. As items were collected, the students reported their grade and homeroom number so a tally of points could be maintained. With 24 homerooms participating, the homeroom with the greatest accumulated points won a pizza party. The party, which was held during a regular school lunch period, helped recognize the contribution of the parent-teacher organization and the efforts of the participants. The school's public address system may be incorporated to help build support during the collection week and at the conclusion of the hunt. The local newspaper, cable company, and school newsletter can also become important partners for this endeavor.

On a designated day, all of the students eagerly brought in everything they had collected. The items were counted, cataloged, and crated according to homeroom by parent volunteers who contributed their time to pick up and deliver. Without the help of parents, the collection of items could take place during science class or homeroom. Students are also quite able to organize an effective force to help with collection and point tallying. Consider enlisting the support of staff to help gather items that are difficult for students to transport.

I got tons of stuff; in fact, the materials I received were only limited by the list that I had assigned. How surprised I was to learn of the community resources that I had never imagined! Items that were not even on the list came in as word got around that our school was finding ways to recycle all types of things. A really big surprise was some of the unexpected goodies that the community contributed, including

- a cutaway automobile battery (salesman's demo)
- several spools of wire (used for electrical experiments and electromagnets)
- oscilloscopes from a commercial lab that had upgraded (used to show characteristics of waves)
- expensive microscopes, boxes of glassware, and lenses, all from businesses that had also upgraded their equipment
- many examples of hand tools (used to demonstrate simple machines)
- a bicycle (used to illustrate gears and other machines)
- fish tubs (used as portable sinks for student experiments)

- small appliances (dissected to show electrical circuits and controls)
- old 45s (to make tops and gyroscopes)
- a tape recorder (used to capture sounds and echoes)

One mom showed up with a cardboard tube much like the ones found in a roll of paper towels. She asked me if I had a use for something like that and I said yes, I could find several uses for the tube—a pinhole camera, a telescope, a roller, or an arm for a mobile. I told her I could come up with a thousand ways to use them. "Good," she said, "that's just about how many I'll bring you." She came the following day with her minivan full of cardboard tubes. I became known as the "scavenger hunt guy" and was an ongoing recipient of equipment from local tech companies that were downsizing or upgrading equipment.

I received electronic equipment, including audio signal generators, incubators, and all types of animal cages and aquaria. What I could not use, I offered to others in our school district, and if no one could use it, I went to colleagues beyond our district. Materials were made available to science teachers first and then to others as well. Most materials were able to

Figure 1

Scavenger hunt request letter

Dear Parents,

To assist the science teachers, your children have been asked to scour your basements, closets, garages, and attics in an effort to locate articles that will help us

- demonstrate concepts to students,
- provide additional materials used in student lab activities, and
- supplement classroom supplies or equipment.

Attached, you will find a list of items the science teachers are looking for, along with a point value. Each item or group of items is worth 5 points. Items with an asterisk (*) are worth 10 points.

Students will be asked to turn in materials on _____ to the organizers at school. Each student will be asked which homeroom they represent to keep track of the items returned. The homeroom that accumulates the greatest point total will be given a pizza party by the parent-teacher organization.

This is a great way to help out the science department, so pitch in if you can!

be stored in teacher classrooms, while larger items were held in the science department storage area or the custodian closet.

The scavenger hunt is a win-win-win situation. My students get access to materials that boost lab investigations. Parents have a chance to contribute and participate, as well as get rid of stuff. I get to spend more of my budget funds on permanent science equipment and not on consumables. A side benefit of a scavenger hunt is the eagerness of the students to see the items they contribute being used in science activities. Many times students have even suggested how materials might be used and brought them in to school. Often they showed more interest in the experiments that incorporated their stuff and contributed more because they developed "bragging rights." Try it. It works.

This article first appeared in the October 2003 issue of Science Scope.

Index